The Warp

D1243577

 lege han
front to

The WARP

A Weaving Reference

Blair Tate

Illustrations by
Carol Keller

Lark Books
Asheville, North Carolina

Published in 1987 and 1991 by
Lark Books
50 College Street
Asheville, North Carolina 28801

10 9 8 7 6 5 4 3 2

ISBN 0-937274-33-X

Designed by Karolina Harris

Illustrations by Carol Keller

Cover photographs by Jeffrey Schift: detail from Rode Stippen, 1976,
by Desiree Scholten van de Riviere

Printed in the United States of America

FOR MY PARENTS

Contents

Acknowledgments   ix

One   WARP BASICS

Introduction   3
1 Yarn   5
    Suitability   5
    Character   8
    Size   23

2 Density/Weave Mechanics   30
    Warp-Face → Warp-Face Balanced   31
    Balanced Weave   38
    Weft-Face Balanced → Weft-Face   48

3 Finishing   55
    Warp as Fringe   56
    Clean Finish Edges   68

Two   HANDLING THE WARP

4 The Loom   79

5 Warping: Dressing the Loom   85
    Basic Warping   86
    Loom Dressing: "Back to Front" vs. "Front to Back"   91
    "Back to Front"   91
    "Front to Back"   98
    Sectional Warping/Beaming   103

6 Weaving/Troubleshooting   110

Appendix A: Burn Test for Fiber Identification   123
Appendix B: Warp Length Calculations   124
Appendix C: Warp/Reed Density Distribution Patterns   125
Appendix D: Metric Equivalents   126
Bibliography   127
Index   129
About the Author   134

Acknowledgments

This book could not have come into being without considerable help from many people. I feel indebted to, and would like to specially thank: all the artists whose work appears in this book, for both the loan of their photographs and negatives, and informative and enjoyable correspondence; Sandy Jones at the American Museum of Natural History, and Katherine Hunter, Marcia Waldman, Naomi Johnson, and Denise Dunn at the Boston Museum of Fine Arts for further assistance with photographs and especially the permission to print them; Pro B & W Service of Boston for their perseverence and skill in coaxing quality from thin negatives; my illustrator Carol Keller for her wonderful drawings and diligence in testing the techniques they describe; photographers Stanley Rowin and Jeffrey Schiff for their patience and enormous contributions to this book; Linda Venator at Van Nostrand Reinhold for easing my way through the publication process; Mildred Constantine for sharing her knowledge of contemporary weavers; my friend Deborah Daw for her astute, helpful criticisms, and often needed votes of confidence; Aija Kusins, Anne Forbes, Mollie Fletcher, Gerhardt Knodel, and Joanne Segal Brandford for generous sharing of technical information; and finally, but far from last, my editor, Irene Demchyshyn, for her faith, encouragement, assistance with the book's design, and suggestion that I write this book in the first place; and my husband, Jeffrey Schiff, without whose loving support, I could not have finished it.

One WARP BASICS

Introduction

When warp and weft are joined, their synthesis is called weaving. Threads are interlaced in perpendicular opposition, to bind them together to form a solidified whole. In off-loom techniques such as plaiting, virtually no distinction is made between the roles played by the two elements of weaving; neither warp nor weft is subject to separate rules nor has a separate function. It is with the introduction of the loom that the identities of warp and weft become distinct.

The differences and similarities, in origin and associative meaning, between the words *warp* and *weft* are worthy of note. *Warp* has its Indo-European roots in *wert-*, *wreit-*, *werbh-*, *werp-*, and *wermi-*. The first four roots all mean to turn, wind, or bend; the last materializes these movements in the form of a worm, a linear creature that moves by undulation. In common usage, warp connotes the bending or twisting of something that was previously straight. It is usually associated with a physical twist in wood or a metaphorical twist in mental perception or attitude. In weaving, with the aid of the loom, the warp starts out as a perfectly straight set of threads. The introduction of the weft compromises its original purity, causing it to bend. In profile, the warp undulates to accommodate the weft.

The words *weft* and *weave* share the same root: *webh-*, which includes Old English *wefan* (to weave), *wefta*, *weft* (cross thread), *webb* (web), and possibly *wafian* (wave), Old Norse *vafra* (waver), and Low German *wabbeln* (sway or wobble). The same word—weaving—applies to both the activity and the result. In action, it refers to a back-and-forth, sideways movement. In popular language, wending one's way through a crowd and a drunkard's stumble are both described as weaving. The intention is for transit to be direct, yet obstacles force detour. In weaving cloth, the weft, the crossing thread, travels over and under, zigzagging around the already existent warp. On a larger scale, the general movement of the weft is back and forth: It is shuttled from side to side, building the cloth row by row. The introduction of the weft is the activity that most defines the weaving process.

Weaving as a product is an integration of numerous elements to form a single complex structure. Terminology referring to this riddles our language: Relationships are interwoven, fates are intertwined, and there are networks of communication. The interconnectedness of the parts is the principal reference, and the image formed is one of solidity.

Weavings are analogous to buildings. Both are products of, and expressive of, the culture that produces them. As such, they are manifestations of logical thought and physical discipline. Both were developed in response to physical need, and at times, both have transcended that function and have been used to serve more spiritual ends. Both have an almost boundless potential for diversity, producing results that can be either ordinary and mundane, or sublime and inspiring.

Weavings and buildings are structures, created by ordered and repeated actions. They develop directionally—respecting gravity, they grow up from the bottom, requiring and building upon secure foundations. Their structures are grids with load-bearing verticals and spanning horizontals. The opposing elements depend on each other: The verticals are joined and stabilized by the horizontals, which in turn rely on the verticals for support. As interdependent as architectural elements, the warp threads would fall apart without the joining weft, and, without the warp, the meandering weft would have no structure through which to weave.

Why then, a book about the warp? How can it be disassociated from the weft? In truth, as the derivation of its name implies, it cannot. This book simply focuses on the warp, recognizing its influence over the whole of the weaving. When weaving is done on a loom, the warp becomes both a single, unified entity, more than the simple sum of its threads, and the first of the two weaving elements. Its primacy, and the inherent requirements it must fulfill, make the warp a distinct subject to be dealt with.

The warp creates the basic field of a weaving, organizing and establishing the ground rules and limits. Once set, it is basically unchangeable, and its influence is unavoidable. It carries within it the potential for the weaving—its scale, texture, and image capability. The weft can only respond to these conditions. It can rebel, but its bid for independence is limited by the structural demand for frequent interaction with the warp. Fortunately, the loom's control forces the warp to act with consistency. The warp becomes a knowable quantity; a clear logic explains its behavior.

The purpose of this book is to examine warp considerations in order to reveal their consequences. One would not construct a building without a plan, yet because of weaving's more intimate scale, it is often impulsively begun. Warp choice is the first step in weaving, yet the ramifications of that choice are frequently overlooked—lost forever in the haste to begin. Without continual reexamination, that choice can become a matter of habit, or convenience, the range of possibilities limited by routine and safe repetition of earlier warps.

This book is intended to encourage reevaluation of methods and materials, and the appropriateness of both. To accomplish this, it is basically structured as two books in one: a general text that discusses technical information, and an interspliced gallery of artworks that manifests some of the many rich and varied possibilities implied by the general text. It is my hope that focusing attention on the basic warp/weft relationships from these two perspectives—the general and the specific—will encourage clear thought and clear work. Within clarity lies the potential for inspiration. In the words of architect Louis Kahn: "Inspiration is the moment of possibility when what to do meets the means of doing it."

1 Yarn

No stage of warp choice should be viewed independently from any other. The type of yarn—its strength, character, size—is as influential to the whole as are the decisions about the manner of its use, its density and corresponding weave type, and the further transformations brought about by weave mechanics. Because writing about the warp is necessarily more linear than either thinking about or choosing one, the various warp considerations will be examined in separate stages.

SUITABILITY

Any essentially linear, flexible material can be a yarn to be used as either the warp or weft element in weaving. For a yarn to be considered eligible for the warp, it must pass three basic commonsense tests:

1. *The yarn should be strong.* It should be able to resist immediate breakage or fraying when a 2- to 3-foot length is snapped with both hands by a quick jerk in opposite directions; and it should remain intact when fairly intense, even strain is applied over the same length. This need for strength is mandated by the point stress imposed by the heddles when the harnesses are raised and lowered, and the strain caused by maintenance of

sufficient tension for the yarns and loom to operate smoothly.

2. *The yarn should be able to withstand abrasion and not suffer textural change* if all the different textures of the yarn are repeatedly scraped between two fingernails. This test simulates the worst possible abrasion that can be inflicted by the reed's continual movement through the yarns.

3. *When stretched, the yarn should remain relatively consistent in length and cross-sectional dimension.* An overly elastic yarn, such as a knitting yarn, can be used, but the final out-of-tension results will show dramatic shrinkage in length and have a puffy appearance, like childhood potholders.

A yarn that meets these requirements should be relatively easy and uncomplicated to work with.

Nonstructural issues, such as color and texture, can figure as importantly in warp choice as the clearer structural concerns do. All manner of difficulties posed by a superficially impractical and generally unacceptable warp yarn may therefore be worth enduring for the final effect.

A weaving yarn that only slightly fails the first two tests—for example, a yarn that breaks on the third or fourth snap rather than the first, or sheds somewhat when scraped, but visually remains the same—can still be used but the following precautions should be taken.

Désirée Scholten van de Rivière
Rode Stippen/1976
wool, linen, cotton, rayon, silk, plastic
55" x 55" (140 x 140 cm.)
Collection: Galerie Nouvelles Images, The Hague

In Rode Stippen *(Red Spotted)*, an open, loosely formed underlying woven web is completely hidden by the lush casade of white warp threads. The visible warp is freed of structural responsibility, and in that sense becomes a supplementary warp. This independent warp is allowed natural movement, subject only to the will of gravity. The unobstructed flow of its rich, varied textures forms the tapestry's surface. The warp's extreme density gives the surface depth, yet makes it visually impenetrable.

Numerous red weft-face woven blocks are scattered across the field. These provide a visual anchor while structurally binding the warp threads, fixing their lateral positions. The red blocks produce a compositional tension through their irregular proximity. Their strict geometry and intense color disassociates them from the plane of warp threads, causing them to project forward. The variation in their sizes suggests that some are closer to the viewer than others. However, all are formed from the tight encasement of the warp yarns and are thus inextricably tied to the warp plane. (Photographs: Jan en Fridtjof, Versnel, Amsterdam, whole view; and Jeffrey Schiff, detail)

When the warp is placed under tension, that tension should be as minimal as possible. Every effort should be made not to stress the yarns during weaving: A dropped shuttle or accidental catch with a finger could cause substantial breakage. The reed should have as few dents as feasible in order to minimize contact with the yarns. Both changing of harnesses and packing of the weft by pulling the beater should be done slowly and gently. If still more delicate handling seems necessary, gentle beating can be done with a smooth sword or batten. Combs and tapestry beaters should be avoided.

If a yarn immediately, unquestionably, fails the first two tests, it should be either rejected or tried again as a double (two yarns that have been wound together and treated as one), triple, quadruple, and so on. Grouping the yarns in this way will increase warp coverage since the multiple threads will tend to lie next to each other, becoming effectively broader. Because the actual yarn thickness is unaffected, it is possible to maintain a more refined, delicate weaving appearance than if a heavier yarn were used.

CHARACTER

The character of a yarn is the combined result of that yarn's construction and the properties inherent in its material.

Construction

Structurally, yarns are either filament or composed of staple fibers. A *filament yarn* is a continuous strand formed by extrusion (the basic process by which a spider generates its web). Many man-made fibers—rayon, nylon, and, in a sense, saran, Lurex, and Mylar—are constructed in this manner. Silk is the only natural filament yarn; it is created by unraveling the silkworm's unbroken cocoon. *Staple fibers* are shorter lengths that are combined by spinning. Cotton, linen, wool, and spun silk (from broken cocoons) fall into this category.

Basic fiber strength is attributable to the length of its staple and degree of twist introduced at the time of spinning. The longer the staple, the stronger the yarn; hence filament yarns are fundamentally the strongest. The degree of twist is determined by measuring the angle between the diagonal slant of the thread's twist and the straight vertical axis of the yarn. Loosely twisted yarns—those with a twist angle of 5°—are considered *soft-spun* and, as the name implies, are generally softer, limper, and weaker. They are barely constructed and rely solely on their staple length for strength. Their limpness allows them to be more influenced by gravity, and they drape well. Soft-spun yarns lack body with which to assert an independent will. Yarns with a twist angle of approximately 20° are considered *medium-twist* and, accordingly, possess a more medium degree of strength. *Hard-spun,* tightly twisted yarns with a twist angle of 30° to 45° are structurally sound and thus strong. Depending on the nature of the fiber, hard-spun yarns will tend toward stiffness. Overspun, extremely twisted yarns, known as *crepe-spun* (twist angle of 65°), look crinkly and tend to kink whenever reduced tension allows. This kinkiness causes them to seem more elastic.

Plying is the process by which two or more already-spun yarns are joined to become a new, single strand. The weakness of the softest-spun, shortest-staple, single-ply yarns is partially counteracted by this type of union: Simple increase in the number of plies increases their cumulative strength and gives them body.

Novelty yarns are those yarns that have been specifically textured in initial spinning and/or in combination with other plies. They are labeled either descriptively (loop, seed, nub, slub, flake) or by their construction (chenille, a woven yarn; gimp, a wrapped yarn; bouclé and ratiné, twined yarns).

Material Content

A wide range of materials are available already processed into yarns suitable for a warp. Choice should be made on the basis of a fiber's specific qualities. For ease and continuity in description, these materials are generally grouped according to their source. Overall, there are two basic categories: the naturally grown and straightforwardly processed plant and animal fibers, and those that are considered man-made, having been synthesized from either organic or inorganic compounds.

The natural yarns predate the man-made ones in discovery and use and, consequently, they are more familiar, known quantities and simpler to discuss. They tend to be more visually consistent, although variations in their processing and finishing can cause functional differences. Cotton is clearly cotton, for example, and does not resemble wool or silk, although its ability to absorb dye or to stretch can be altered by different processing techniques.

In marked contrast, a great many of the man-made fibers can be remarkably varied both in appearance and behavior. The same fiber can be manufactured with qualities that are unique and distinctive or intentionally chameleonlike. For instance, nylon is the fiber of fishing line, but it can also be made to resemble cotton, wool, or rayon. Hence, discussion of the man-made fibers can never be absolute but must always be qualified. These fibers have been invented and continue to be developed for a multitude of virtues, versatility among them. By necessity, then, descriptions of only some of the basic qualities of the man-made yarns most frequently used in handweaving will follow.

PLANT FIBERS

COTTON, culled from the fruit of the cotton plant, is a relatively strong, soft, and pliable fiber. It is spun from either long (greater than 1-inch) or short (less than 1-inch) staple fibers. The longer the staple, the smoother, silkier, more crisp or "hard" looking the fiber appears. American Pima, Sea Island, and Egyptian cottons are renowned for their extremely long staples (approximately 1½ inches) and are highly prized for their polished hand (or tactile quality). Because they are very strong, they can be spun very finely. For example, American Pima is used principally for sewing thread. In contrast, short staple American Upland and Asiatic (i.e., Indian) cottons are softer, fuzzier, duller, and drier in appearance; in character they seem less refined and more humble. These are the cottons that can be brushed after weaving to achieve a flannellike softness.

Both the look and action of cotton fiber can be al-

tered by the basic way it is processed and finished. Generally speaking, cotton shrinks considerably when wet and is fairly inelastic when dry. It will elongate only slightly under tension and usually revert to its original length once the tension has been relaxed. But if tension (of the sort exerted by the downward pull of gravity on a vertically hung fabric) is protracted, cotton's growth ceases to reverse itself. Compactness of weave construction can minimize the inherent tendency for stretch, and submersion in water can cause shrinkage, either restoring or reducing the yarn's original length. *Mercerization,* an industrial process involving immersion of the yarn in caustic soda, offsets both growth and shrinkage and essentially fixes the length of the yarn. It is a finish that seems to harden the yarn, making it stronger and more lustrous (thus more desirable and expensive). On the other hand, a related process, *slack mercerization,* although giving the yarn a similar appearance, will have the opposite effect. Both slack mercerizing and crepe-spinning increase the yarn's elasticity beyond its natural ability.

Cotton is a highly absorbent fiber, able to soak up twice its weight in water. Tightness of yarn twist will slightly reduce this absorbability while slack twist and openness of weave will encourage it. Because of its natural absorbency, cotton readily accepts dye (more brilliantly after mercerization) and dries quite slowly. If stored damp, it is susceptible to rot and mildew. Cotton bleaches well but will lose strength and yellow (from oxidation) if subjected to prolonged exposure to direct sunlight. Cotton is extremely durable and holds up well through repeated washings. It gains more strength when wet than any other natural fiber (its wet strength is 30 percent higher than its normal dry strength).

Essentially, cotton is an exceedingly versatile fiber. Its widespread use in clothing and functional fabrics attests to its many virtues.

LINEN is a strong, stubborn bast fiber extracted from the stalk of the flax plant. Its strength among the natural fibers is second only to that of silk, and it is two to three times stronger than cotton. Linen has a relatively stiff, crisp hand, and abounds with body, but it notably lacks resilience. This shortcoming has earned

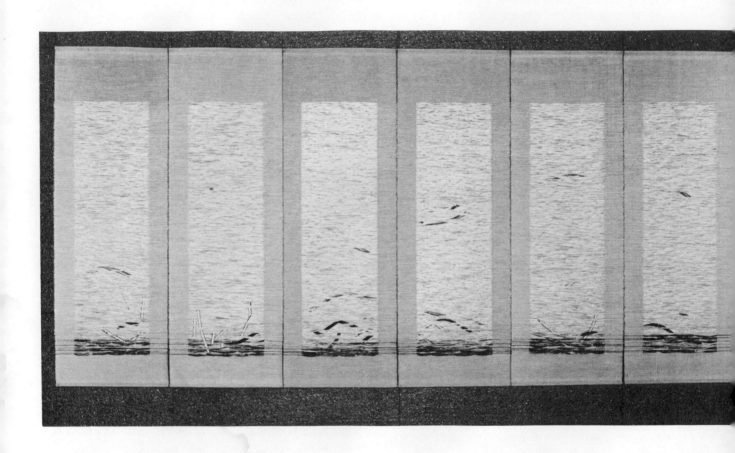

Cynthia Schira
View to the East/*1976*
cotton, cotton ikat-dyed tapes
84" x 180" (213 x 457 cm.)
Collection: Cabot, Cabot, and Forbes, Boston

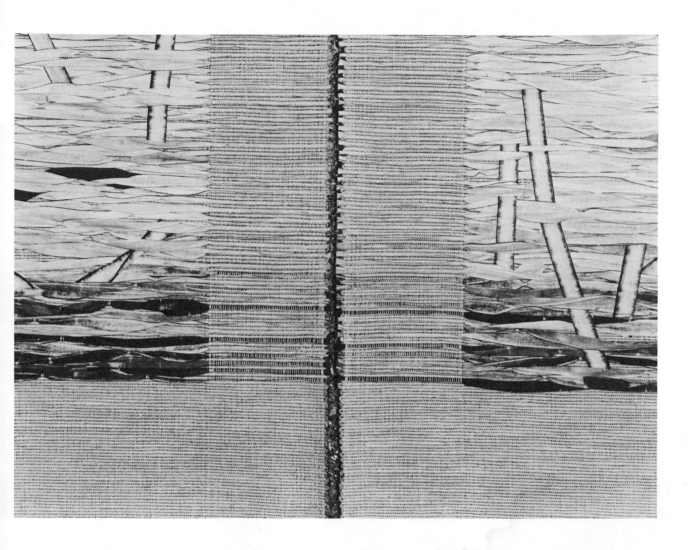

Oriental in quality and character of line, View to the East *is composed of separately woven, juxtaposed panels. Its proportions, lowered visual center, and pictorial nature refer to Japanese hanging scrolls, but their synthesis to form a continuous image is nontraditional.*

Despite the physical interruption between panels, the work reads as a whole. The slight extension of the weft tapes beyond the woven warp's edge suggests a continuous weft from panel to panel, encouraging visual fusion between them.

Each panel consists of a central area differentiated from its surrounding border by textural contrast. In this center, supplementary weft tapes are permitted spirited movement, freed from the warp's constraint. The subdued sense of uniformity and neutrality in the borders is directly attributable to warp decisions. The natural-colored mercerized cotton is humble in character and nonintrusive. Its warp-face balanced sett overrules and homogenizes the woven-in weft tapes. The characteristic molding of warp-face density yarns to the weft's contour creates textural horizontal ribs. This ribbing reduces the contrast between the thinner weft areas (at top and bottom of each panel) and the far bulkier weft tapes (at the sides). (Photographs: Stanley Rowin, Boston) it the reputation for being "unforgiving." Linen seems capable of modest elongation at the slightest provocation, but, unlike cotton, the stretch is irreversible. It also has a memory for all stages of its manipulation and, as a result, must be treated correctly. As a warp, linen should be beamed accurately and kept under tight tension. During weaving, these yarns should be handled as though they were fragile: care should be taken to see that the edge threads are not stretched by the continuous removal and insertion of weft, and that a clear shed is maintained to minimize accidental catches by the thrown shuttle. Additionally, in very dry climates, and particularly with very thin yarns, it is sometimes advisable to keep a linen warp damp to reduce breakage where lack of moisture encourages brittleness in the yarn. The warp can be dampened by draping a slightly wet cloth across the threads where they pass over the back beam. This precaution, however, although helpful to the linen, can be damaging to the loom because it will encourage rust in any rustable parts (such as steel heddles or reed) that the damp yarn touches. The advent of rust in either the heddles or the reed may stain the yarn. (*Note:* You can avoid the problem of rust by using aluminum heddles with a stainless steel reed.)

In spite of this need for special treatment, linen's unique qualities make it a wonderful and very singular warp yarn. There is no substitute for linen's remarkable body—its almost wiry nature underscores and punctuates the woven structure.

Linen, like cotton, is produced from different-length staple fibers. The spinning of long staple (10 to 30 inches) creates *line* yarns; these are considered premium quality because they are stronger and visually more uniform. *Tow* yarns, made from short staple (less than 10 inches) and waste (scrap ends), are coarse and irregular in appearance. *Demi-line* is the middle-line, medium-priced, seldom-offered hybrid of the two grades.

Linen can be either wet-spun, a process that subjects the fiber to 160° F to 180° F water in order to soften the natural gums and align the individual fibers, or dry spun. Wet-spun linen is smoother, more dimensionally uniform, crisper, and harder looking. Dry-spun linen is fuzzier, hairier, and slubbier.

Linen is available in various stages of refinement: *in the gray,* natural, or bleached and/or dyed. Linen in the gray, or simply *gray linen,* is essentially unfinished, still in its "field" state with impurities left in. It is desirable for its grayish tan color, but is more susceptible to rot and mildew. Wet-spun gray linen maintains some (a bit less) of the color, while also eliminating some of the impurities. *Natural* (sometimes called boiled) *linen* has been boiled and scoured to remove impurities. It is left with a characteristic off-white, slightly beige, or pale gray natural color. *Bleached linen* is pure white. Linen generally accepts dye less vibrantly than mercerized cotton does, with some colors, notably reds, tending to be duller.

Linen is relatively sensitive to the environment and is susceptible to temperature and, particularly, humidity change. It will absorb moisture and stretch if given the opportunity (gauzy weaves will accentuate the stretch, while tight weave constructions help counter it) and as mentioned earlier, will become brittle to the point of fracture if denied all humidity. Linen withstands direct sunlight better than cotton does: In comparable conditions, linen's deterioration will be considerably slower.

Linen's versatility is in its broad range of manufacture, which yields visual character ranging from fibrous to a dull sheen, slightly wiry to stiff. At its extreme, linen can seem almost paper- or wood-like.

RAMIE, also known as *Rhea* or *China Grass,* is a bast fiber that in many respects is comparable to linen. It is exceptionally strong, stiff, lustrous, absorbent, and inelastic. It bleaches to a bright white, dyes well, and has a high resistance to mildew and rot. Ramie is as strong as linen but weighs approximately half its weight. Although ramie grows more quickly, its processing is more costly and, as a result, there is less fiber commercially available.

HEMP, another bast fiber, is so similar to linen that if judged strictly by appearances, the two would be confused. Hemp is extracted from the stalk of the marijuana plant and, consequently, is not cultivated (and is somewhat hard to find) in the United States. In contrast with both linen and ramie, hemp cannot be bleached without severely damaging the fiber. It is impervious to salt water and, like ramie, resists rot. Hemp resembles linen in stiffness, strength, and durability.

JUTE, from the jute plant, is the black sheep of the bast fibers. It is probably the most common and inexpensive natural fiber, has considerably longer yet weaker fibers than linen, is unbleachable and inelastic, and deteriorates rapidly in water. Jute has a distinctive smell and both weakens and yellows in a relatively short time. It is primarily available as a coarse, fuzzy, dry, "gray" yarn—often with impurities left in. Occasionally more linenlike, refined, stable, paler-color fibers can be found. Jute's availability and low cost make it useful for experimentation.

SISAL is obtained from the leaf of the agave cactus. Its relatively straight, pale yellow fibers are silky in appearance, but coarse and abrasive to the touch because of their many short ends similar to split ends in hair. Because of the fiber's strength and bite, it is principally used for rope, packing twine, and brush bristles. Sisal is stiff, wiry, and inelastic. It can be both bleached and dyed, but these transformations tend to be short-lived; oxidation of the fiber is rapid, causing the bleached white to yellow and the dyed colors to fade.

ABACA, produced from the leaves of a plant in the banana family, is sometimes called Manila hemp. Its fiber is strong, resilient, and dyeable. Abaca is generally sisallike, but more refined.

COIR is a stiff, coarse, and elastic fiber taken from the outer husk of the coconut. It is commonly used in ship cordage and door mats because it is unaffected by salt water.

RAFFIA (also spelled raphia) is a relatively strong but inelastic, broad, ribbonlike fiber taken from the leaf of the raffia palm. Its naturally short lengths—approximately three to four feet—are sometimes spun together and sometimes knotted to form a longer, continuous strand. These knots can be problematic in a warp because they may catch in either the heddles or reed and cause breakage. It is helpful to use a low-density reed (one with fewer dents and larger spaces)

and either large, round-eyed wire heddles or string heddles when working with a knotted raffia warp.

PAPER YARNS, synthesized from cellulosic fibers (the basic constituents in plant tissues), are generally either tightly rolled (spiraling) or flat and ribbonlike. They are stiff and inelastic and have a profile that is sharp and crisp. In appearance, paper yarns can be either dry and mat, or wet and glossy if they have been waxed or varnished. Waxed finishes tend to soften and feel gummy if subjected to enough heat, and if the wax melts, it can spread into, and stain, adjacent yarns.

Paper yarns are somewhat unusual and are quite distinctive as warp yarns, and they may require special handling. Manipulation by the loom can cause scarring and breakage. In weaving paper yarns, the raising and lowering of the harnesses causes the heddles to inflict a point stress on each yarn, which may temporarily or permanently crimp it. If the paper is delicate, this repeated strain can cause it to break. Reducing the overall warp tension may minimize this danger. Scarring can also be caused by the bending of the yarns around the squarish edge of both the breast and back beams: padding or, even better, rounding of the beams (by attaching large half-round wooden or metal pieces with matching diameters to the beams' thickness) can completely eliminate this problem.

ANIMAL FIBERS

WOOL is a highly elastic protein fiber grown on the backs and bellies of sheep. Different grades and character of wool come from different breeds of sheep as well as from different parts of the fleece. In general, wool has a dry, dull hand and is both physically and visually warmer than any of the plant fibers. Wool fibers have loft, which contributes to their physical warmth and effectiveness as heat and sound insulators. This loft gives them a less specific, almost hazy profile that enables juxtaposed colors to visually blend. Whenever the fiber's loft is particularly high, brushing the woven surface after weaving will further enhance this blendability. In this respect, wool is in extreme contrast with mercerized cotton and wet-spun linen: the crisp nature of those plant fibers (and particularly linen) encourages distinctions between threads, whereas the

Anne Wilson
Swag/1982
linen, abaca, rayon, graphite, acrylic medium
49" x 12" x 7" (124 x 30 x 18 cm.)

Swag's *initial drama is in its strikingly formal yet casual suspension—the densely woven, weighty cloth hangs vertically as one would expect while swaying in seeming defiance of gravity.*

The piece is created from a single, long, relatively wide woven band. Its dense, warp-face structure gives the cloth the necessary body to retain vitality along its smooth curve. The sideways sway is the result of very gradual shaping of the band during weaving. The changing angle of the weave is so subtle that it never really reveals itself; it physically, but never visually, deviates from the usual right angle intersection of warp and weft.

The band is hung in a manner that reveals both surfaces of the cloth, exposing and contrasting their remarkably different natures. One side of the fabric is uniformly textured because of the band's warp-face construction and has been further homogenized by impregnation with acrylic medium and graphite. This treatment hardens the surface, giving it a metallic sheen and a shieldlike quality. The reverse side is surprising. Supplementary weft elements introduce a strictly geometric, yet variably patterned checkerboard while also providing a bristling and uncontrollable counterpoint. (Photographs: Mary Jo Toles, Chicago)

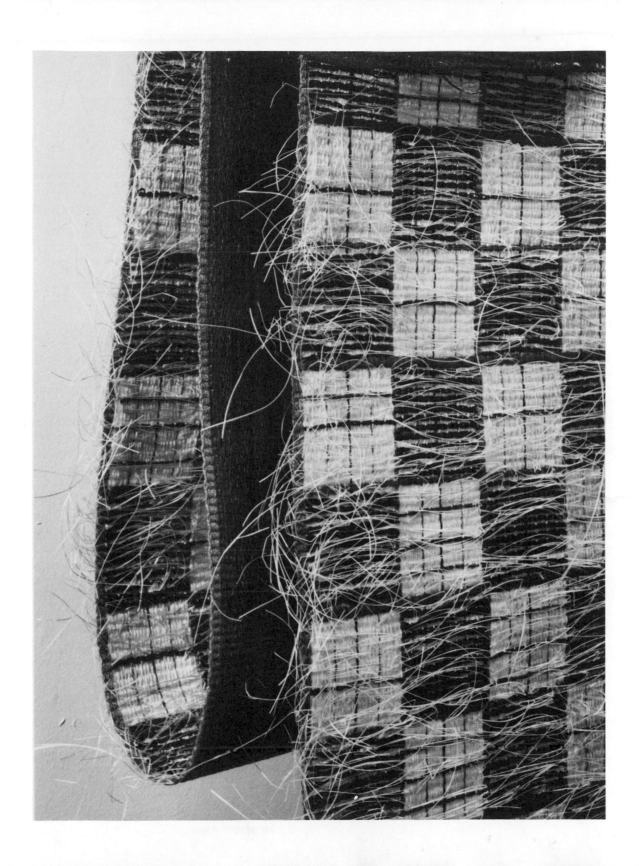

softness of wool can be used to blur edges (or with brushing, even obscure them).

Wool has the most elasticity of all the natural fibers, with a stretch capacity of approximately 25 percent. This quality can be either accentuated or diminished by yarn and weave construction. Heavy, vertically hung, loosely woven panels can grow rather impressively over a period of time. To counter this, a tight weave structure is imperative.

Wool fibers are divided into two basic categories: worsted and woolen. *Worsted* is spun from long staple fiber (from 3 to 5 inches). It is more tightly spun, stronger, harder, more durable, often finer (due to basic strength), more dimensionally even, smoother, and yet scratchier to the touch than short-staple woolen fiber is. (The degree of scratchiness is to a certain extent relative. Some people develop a hypersensitivity which, upon contact, induces a hystamine reaction in the skin.) *Woolen* fiber is usually loosely spun, fluffier, and softer.

Wool has a relatively low tensile strength (lowest of the natural fibers), which is partially offset by its high elasticity and can also be compensated for by increased twist. The harder the twist, the stronger the wool becomes. Rug wool, made from coarse, low-grade, relatively inelastic and weak fibers, is strong and resistant to abrasion because of its hard twist and multiple ply.

Wool has natural crease resistance and is more flame retardant than either cotton or linen but is susceptible to damage from moths, particularly when soiled. Wool fibers must be cleaned gently; they lose about one-quarter of their strength when wet, and if shocked by sudden immersion in hot water, they will mat and begin to felt. Mothproofing eliminates the risk of moth damage.

Wool is an extremely absorbent fiber, despite its initial appearance to the contrary. On first contact, water will bead on the surface and can be easily brushed off. Some wools are processed to retain some of their natural grease, or lanolin, and these yarns are truly water-repellent (the yarn used in authentic fisherman sweaters is an example). With time, however, most wools can absorb between 20 and 30 percent of

The intersecting arcs in Drie Bogen *(Three Curves) are each lumbering, heavy shapes, yet when combined, they have a frolicsome, gestural quality. The weightiness of the work, due to each strip's breadth and to large-scale, textural materials, is in contradiction with its seeming weightlessness, suggested by the strips' gravity-defying movement. The pretzellike configuration contributes to the tapestry's playfulness at the same time as it creates a memorable, almost still, emblematic image.*

Drie Bogen *is created from three, separately woven weft-face bands. At the time of weaving, the loom-controlled warp yarns were all parallel, but only wedge shaped sections were woven. After removal from the loom, the warp was pulled, cinching the woven segments together. By using a weft-face weave, which calls for no warp interaction, the warp threads could be more simply drawn through the web. In addition, the weft-face weaving rigidified the structure, keeping the shapes crisp, and enabled the horizontal striping to be thinner, allowing for more subtle shading effects. (Photograph: Maarten D'Oliveira, Amsterdam)*

Herman Scholten
Drie Bogen/*1973*
wool, sisal, abaca
67" x 122" (170 x 310 cm.)
Collection: Water Company, Rijn-Kennemerland—
Nieuwegein

their own weight without feeling damp, 50 percent without becoming saturated, and, when thoroughly soaked, will have absorbed approximately four times their dry weight. Wool both shrinks and stretches, and if hung wet, the stretch will be considerable under the increased burden. Wet wool has a very distinctive odor. Wool dyes brilliantly, dries slowly, and is less prone to mildew than either cotton or linen.

MOHAIR is spun from long staple (9 to 12 inches) hairs of the Angora goat. It is smoother and more cross-sectionally uniform than wool, and is exceptionally springy, as well as being the strongest of the animal hair fibers. Mohair neither shrinks nor felts as readily as wool and it dyes well.

CASHMERE is made from the short, soft underhairs of the Tibetan (or Kashmir) goat. The longer fleece hairs are more akin to ordinary goat hair, which is wiry and coarse. Cashmere fibers are delicate, light (about half the weight of wool), extremely soft, and have high loft, making them very good insulators. Their fragility makes them less suitable for warp and less durable than wool.

CAMEL'S HAIR comes in two basic grades: the soft, silken underhair, which is more refined, and the longer-staple, coarser outerhair, which is considerably less luxuriant. The short staple underhairs, called noils, are pale tan in color and moderately strong but are easily weakened by abrasion. Sometimes this more delicate fiber is blended with wool to produce a strong, light, exceptionally warm and durable fiber. The coarse, strong outerhairs are deeper colored, ranging from reddish brown to brownish black. They need no reinforcement and are often used in cordage and rugs.

LLAMA, produced by a type of camel, is a brownish colored fiber that resembles camel's hair. Like the camel, the llama has strong outerhairs and softer noil inner ones. The more delicate noil fibers are often blended with other animal hair yarns, contributing the qualities of resilience, lightness, and durability.

ALPACA, from a type of llama specially bred for its luxurious fiber, also has two basic grades: harder, stronger outerhairs, and more delicate, silken inner noils. The ratio of their combination determines the yarn's properties. Alpaca ranges in color from white to reddish brown to gray to black. The fiber is quite soft, lustrous, very warm, water-repellent, and, depending on the combination, fairly strong.

VICUNA comes from a llama like, but considerably smaller animal. Its fiber is soft, delicate, tan to orange-brown in color, highly elastic, and extraordinarily expensive because of the rareness, wildness, and relative inaccessibility of the beast.

GOAT HAIR and HORSEHAIR (from the manes and tails of horses) seem like anomalies since generally softness and warmth are associated with animal hair fibers. Both are strong, coarse, exceptionally stiff fibers, traditionally used for reinforcement in upholstery and coat tailoring.

SILK is the fiber that results from unwinding the filament secreted by the silkworm for its cocoon. The luxuriant protein fiber exhibits very different characteristics, depending on its source and manufacture.

Traditional *cultivated silk* (also called *filament silk*) comes from the unbroken twin filaments of a mulberry-leaf-fed silkworm. It is milky white in color and extremely fine, has a smooth and polished hand, and is exceedingly strong—stronger than its cross-sectional equivalent in wire. Its fineness is such that generally three to ten separate cocoons are unwound and re-wound, or "reeled" together, to produce a thicker, commercially usable yarn. The reeled silk is then subjected to a process called "throwing," in which the yarns are again drawn out, but at this point, given some twist. The degree, direction, and type of twist determine the yarn's elasticity.

Spun silk, often mistakenly called raw silk, refers to the spinning of shorter-staple silk fibers. These come from damaged cocoons (where the moth has been allowed to escape in order to continue its life and perpetuate silk cultivation) and from the cocoon's unreelable ends. Spun silks are less strong, less naturally elastic, more textural (often having slubs), and more cottonlike in their dry-seeming dullness than thrown silks are.

The term *noil* is applied to spun silk scraps. *Silk*

noil is generally cream colored with dark flecks and has a dry but slightly sticky feel from gum residues left in the yarn.

Wild silk is a type of spun silk produced from the filaments of silkworms fed on oak leaves. The hatching moths break their filaments, necessitating spinning to create the yarn. The color of wild silk ranges from cream to warm brown. *Tussah,* a particular kind of wild silk, is a soft, golden brown.

All silks dye readily and intensely, and if not placed in strong light, the color will be reasonably permanent. Wild silks are generally appreciated for their natural color and so are left undyed. Silk is absorbent, capable of holding between 10 and 30 percent of its weight in water, and is not particularly susceptible to mildew. It waterspots easily, but unless precluded by some special industrial finishes, complete immersion will eradicate the spots. Wet silk shrinks slightly, but it can be stretched by ironing to recover its original length. The extent of its elasticity, as mentioned earlier, is variable. In general, stretched silk will slowly return to its former length, over time. Although inherently stronger than cotton or wool, silk is weakened more quickly by prolonged exposure to direct sunlight than either of these fibers are.

MAN-MADE FIBERS

RAYON is considered man-made because its basic fiber does not occur naturally. It is not a true synthetic yarn, however, because its raw materials—wood pulp and cotton linters—are natural. Rayon is formed by extrusion in a manner similar to that used for silk and could be generally described as being silklike. In keeping with the analogy, its fibers are sometimes cut into shorter staple lengths and spun into yarn. There are two main types of rayon, each with somewhat different characteristics as a result of the numerous options in processing and finishing:

Viscose rayon's tensile strength varies considerably, ranging from fibers that are stronger than wool but weaker than cotton (40 to 70 percent weaker still when wet) to specially produced high tenacity yarns that are stronger than silk. Viscose rayon is generally more elastic than cotton or linen, but less than silk or wool.

It stretches considerably under tension and shrinks back slowly, but not completely, when tension has been released. Because it has a heavy hand, it drapes well. It can have a smooth, wet, liquid look or, in its spun version, can resemble fuzzy wool or cotton. Viscose rayon can be formed already colored, which will make it fast, or it can be dyed. Its absorbency is high and causes considerable stretch, which fortunately reverses with evaporation; but it shrinks significantly and repeatedly with frequent washing, although it can be industrially preshrunk. It is fairly resistant to damage from direct sunlight, particularly when dyed, but, like cotton, is susceptible to mildew.

The second type of rayon—*high-wet modulus rayon*—was developed to reduce the severity of viscose rayon's strength loss when wet. High-wet modulus rayon is basically like viscose rayon, except that it is stronger (particularly when wet) and less elastic (with elasticity more comparable to that of cotton). It temporarily waterspots like silk.

NYLON was the first truly synthetic fiber to be manmade. Its raw materials are hydrogen, nitrogen, oxygen, and carbon arranged in a long polyamide chain. Structurally, nylon yarn can be produced from monofilament or multifilament, or it can be spun from cut staple lengths. Nylon is one of the lightest and strongest yarns made and, depending on its construction, one of the most elastic and abrasion resistant as well. It is one of the, if not *the,* most versatile yarns and is said to have more end uses than any other fiber. Nylon can be either textured or smooth, does not lose strength with age, can be heat set to take on a form, does not change shape when wet, and is not very absorbent and dries quickly (with the exception of spun nylon, which is more absorbent and dries slowly). It is virtually unaffected by intense light, mildew, and insects.

Nylon monofilament, or fishing line, has a variable stretch depending on its manufacture. If stretched for a limited time, it will recover completely. Over an extended period, however, its retraction will be slight. Nylon's expected strength is usually given very specifically in pound test information. The surface of monofilament is so smooth as to be slippery, and conse-

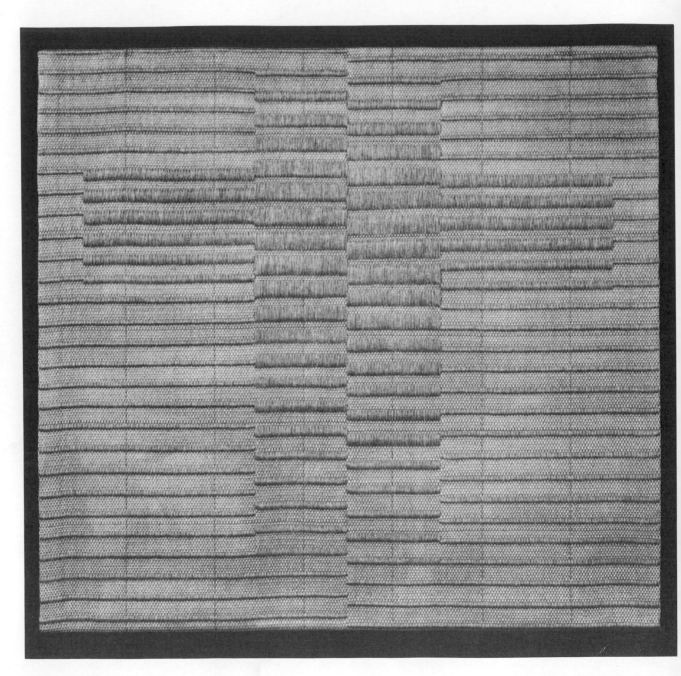

Anne McCarthy Forbes
Manta #4/1982
linen, metallic
34½" x 35" (88 x 90 cm.)

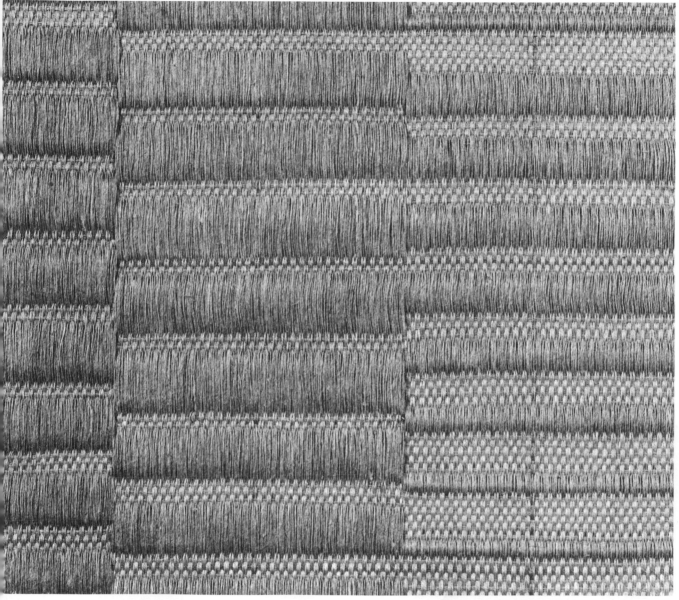

In Manta #4, *the fractured cross image barely distinguishes itself from the ribbed monochromatic field. It is defined solely by the contrast of the supplementary warp emerging en masse from the balanced ground weave. Like a video screen composed of parallel bands of tone, the image results from the accumulation of thicker and thinner lines of warp brocade raised above the surface of the woven ground. The horizontal lines break their continuity as sections shift out of phase with each other to form a separate rhythm. The weaving seems to rupture at the central vertical seam, as if the two halves have drifted apart. Yet the uniform ground weave continues throughout the field, and the overall rectangular shape remains intact. (Photographs: David Caras, Boston)*

quently standard knots are hard to form and secure. (Because of this, DuPont produces a pamphlet simply called "How to Tie Dependable Fishing Line Knots," which is available for the asking.)

Spun nylon is softer, fuzzier, warmer, less elastic, and even more abrasion resistant than filament nylon. Paradoxically, spun nylon pills when washed, requiring more gentle handling when wet.

POLYPROPYLENE is an olefin, or paraffin, fiber. It is the lightest of all fibers, is fairly strong, and has good abrasion resistance. Structurally, it can be made of monofilament or multifilament, slit into thin sheets, or spun from cut shorter-staple lengths. Polypropylene is less elastic than nylon and will stretch permanently if stressed over time. It is virtually nonabsorbent and cannot be successfully dyed, but can be formed with a limited range of colors. Polypropylene is weakened by sunlight but is immune to mildew and insects. Its strength and nonabsorbency explain its frequent use in producing marine ropes.

SARAN is a fiber that is chemically synthesized from extruded polymer compounds of ethylene and chlorine. It is somewhat stiff, yet has a fair degree of stretch and slow recovery. Saran is stronger than wool and viscose rayon, but weaker than the other natural fibers, and is known for its abrasion resistance. It is nonabsorbent, hence basically undyeable (although some newer sarans can be dyed), can be formed with color, which will then be colorfast, and is immune to damage from direct sunlight, mildew, insects, and bacteria. Saran weakens and melts from heat, but is basically nonflammable. It is unaffected by age. Saran is standardly used in screening and outdoor furniture because of its imperviousness to weather.

METALLIC fibers can be finely drawn pure metals, extruded and sliced sheet materials that are spiral-wrapped around a core (gimp), or sheet materials sandwiched between layers of plastic or polyester film.

Gold, silver, copper, aluminum, and other metals are used in the making of filament metallics. These are generally heavier, less flexible, and susceptible to climatic change. Where the metallic yarn is a gimp, the character of the core will influence its strength and

elasticity, and the metal will determine its color.

The primary metal used in the sheet metallic sandwiches is aluminum foil, with color added either to the coating or adhesive in lamination. The color remains fixed and brilliant because of the protective coating. *Lurex* and *Metlon* are trade names for metallic yarns of this sort. The coating used to give the yarn most strength and flexibility is a polyester film called *Mylar*.

A variation on these yarns consists of a Mylar core coated with aluminum particles and sandwiched between outer layers of Mylar. Yarns of this type are lighter, brighter, and more lustrous.

In general, Mylar-coated metallics are strong and very lightweight. Their color can be either intense or muted; their surface either dull or shiny; and they can be manufactured to be reflective, transparent, translucent, or opaque. They are cross-sectionally flat and, if twisted, will change both in texture and in light reflectivity. In handling, they are flexible, but will become brittle with prolonged exposure to heat. Mylar-coated metallics have a fair amount of elasticity and hence stretch under tension, but almost completely retract once that tension has been released. They have body and hold a form well.

WIRE, in contrast, is stiff and totally inelastic, and can be brittle. Because of wire's rigidity a fabric plane woven with it can be bent to hold a form, a quality not generally expected of cloth.

Wire is usually smooth, can be plain or coated with rubber or plastic, and can have either a shiny or dull finish. The composition of wire's exposed surface will dictate its behavior over time and determine whether it will tarnish, rust, corrode, or not. For practical purposes, only fairly thin, somewhat flexible wire should be considered for use as a warp because a wire warp can be rough on the loom. If the wire is too stiff, tight tension may prevent the lifting of harnesses.

On the other hand, the loom can be equally harsh on a wire warp. When the harnesses are raised and lowered, the point stress exerted by the heddles may crimp the wire, causing it to weaken or break. Initial tying up of the warp carries a similar risk of point fracture. And finally, the warp may be uniformly scarred as it passes around the breast beam. Reduction in warp tension may both help the loom's functioning and lessen strain on the warp. Rounding of the breast and back beams by addition of half-cylinders with diameters the size of the beams' thickness will avert some of the scarring.

In addition to the above-mentioned yarns, there are countless other, intriguing, man-made ones—often sold in nameless odd lots. Each should be tested for suitability and put through whatever subsequent trials—washing, pressing, hanging, exposure to direct sunlight, and so on—that will be expected of the finished article. You can also attempt a diagnosis, aided by analysis of a burning, and burnt, portion of the fiber (see Appendix A).

SIZE

The size or cross-sectional dimension of a yarn gives the weaving a fundamental scale. Size and proximity of yarns (density) establish the possibilities for the weave type.

Yarn size is given in numbers. For all fibers composed of staple lengths, the higher the number, the finer the thread. For example, in cotton, number designations between 1 and 20 indicate a coarse yarn; between 20 and 60, a medium to fine thread; number 60 and above, fine to very fine. Standard cotton sewing thread is either a number 50 or 60. A second number, if given, usually follows a slash and indicates the number of plies. (In worsted, this sequence is often reversed: i.e., two plies of #60 yarn are written 2/60, rather than the customary 60/2.)

Each type of yarn has a set quantity of yards per pound. The basic term for this yardage per pound factor changes with the different fibers. Cotton is designated in *counts*; linen in *leas*; woolens are spun according to either the *cut* or *run* system; and worsted is counted in *counts*. Table 1-1 gives the standard length, in yards, of 1 pound of each of these fibers.

When this factor is multiplied by the yarn size number and then divided by the ply, the resulting sum indicates the approximate number of yards per pound for that size thread. For example, a 10/2 linen is com-

Table 1-1. Fiber Designations and Length Standards

Fiber	Counting Term/ System	Yards/ Pound Factor
Cotton Spun silk All man-made staple fibers (except acrylic)	Count	840
Linen Wool	Lea	300
woolen	Cut Run	300 1,600
worsted worsted blends 100% staple acrylics	Count	560
Filament yarns silk rayon nylon	Denier	4,464,400.5 (9000 m./ gm.)

Metric Conversions

To convert *yards/pound to meters/kilo,* first find the approximate numbers of meters/pound by multiplying the yards/pound factor by .9, then multiply that figure by 2.2.

To convert *meters/kilo into yards/pound,* divide the meters/kilo by 2.2, which will give you the meters/pound, then divide this sum by .9.

Note: The factors used above are approximations. They are rounded off from the following measurement equivalents:

1 yard = .9144 meters 1 meter = 1.093 yards
1 pound = 453.59 grams 1 kilo   = 2.2049 pounds

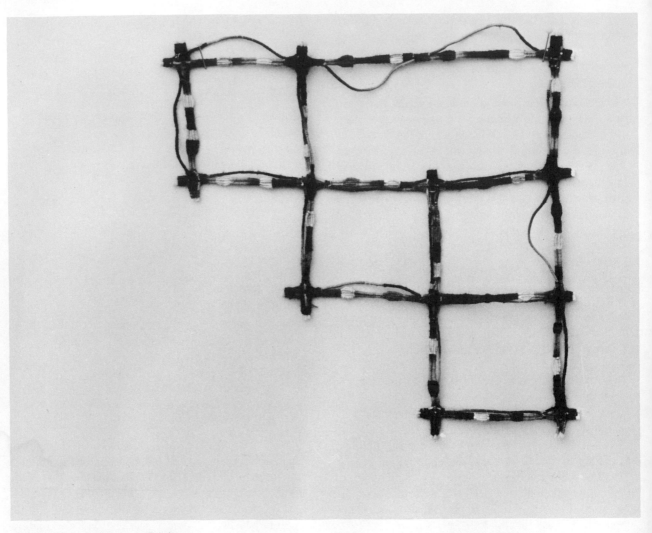

Désirée Scholten van de Rivière
Skyline/*1978*
wool, silk, cotton
8" x 8" (20 x 20 cm.)
Collection: Benno Premsela, Amsterdam

Skyline, *a miniature work, is, in a sense, all graphic outline. As its name imp'ies, it makes reference to man-made grid constructions—buildings, frames, window mullions, urban street maps, as well as weaving. It is made up of wrapped warps and weft-face woven narrow strips that are regularly interwoven through each other.*

The stiff, wrapped warps are given additional length, allowing them more fluid and independent movement, in contrast with the pure grid geometry of the strips. Each strip is woven with finely scaled weft, which refines the weaving, encasing much heavier warp, which gives the work a physicality. Bold, horizontal bands of color on each strip produce the effect of a nearly uniform, finer-scaled block grid. These details sometimes correspond with each other, and sometimes do not, creating a liveliness and spontaneity that activates the overall structure. (Photograph: Robert Schlingemann, Amsterdam) posed of two, plied, size 10 (usually written as 10/1) linen threads. The 10 indicates the fineness of the yarn—ten times finer than a single lea—and implies 10 × 300, or 3,000 yards per pound. However, because there are two threads, and not just one, their combined weight is double what a single yarn's would be. To keep the total weight at one pound, the two yarns' length will have to be halved (10 × 300)/2, yielding 1,500 yards/pound. A 5/1 linen will have 5 × 300, or 1,500 yards per pound—an equivalent length and thickness to the 10/2 linen. The 5/1 and the 10/2 will look different, but as far as their size is concerned, they can be used interchangeably.

These yarn size designations are meant for comparisons only within a specific fiber type. The numbers used in designating spun silk, although sharing the same terminology as cotton, for some unfathomable and unfortunate reason have a different meaning. Whereas a 60/2 cotton is a two-ply #60 cotton thread, equal in size and weight to a #30 cotton yarn (both having 25,200 yards/pound), a 60/2 spun silk indicates two plies of #120 yarns, resulting in the equivalent of a #60 weight silk yarn (with 50,400 yards/pound).

Filament yarns, because of their potential for extreme fineness, are sized according to a completely different system. In the *denier* system, 9,000 meters of fiber weigh 1 gram. This seemingly peculiar equivalency is based on the weight of a denier—a small, eighth- to eighteenth-century French coin that weighed 50 milligrams, as did 450 meters of silk yarn. With deniers, the smaller the number, the finer the yarn. A #1 denier yarn yields 9,000 meters per gram, while a #10 indicates a 900-meter length. Translating this into yards/pound will make the extreme fineness of a denier more immediately understandable: 1 denier of yarn measures 4,464,400.5 yards in length; 10 deniers equal 446,440.05 yards.

When denier yarn sizes are written with slash divisions between numbers—for example, 13/15—this indicates the size range of the thread. The thickness of silk varies because the filament extruded by the silkworm is not consistent. The actual yardage per pound can therefore never be accurately determined, although a close estimate of length can be figured by using the larger number.

One final, completely different system for yarn size designations should be mentioned briefly. Known as the *Tex system,* it was developed in an attempt to standardize the size designations for all yarns. Like metric measurements in the United States or Esperanto worldwide, its generalized use has not yet come about in the manner predicted at its inception.

The Tex system is based on 1 tex weighing 1 gram and measuring 1 kilometer. The higher the tex number, the greater the weight, and the thicker the yarn (Table 1-2). The tex number can be used as a common denominator for ascertaining equivalent yarn sizes between different-material yarns.

If, however, you have the two fibers in hand, their relative sizes can be more simply compared. To do this, wrap each yarn uniformly and solidly—neither overlapping nor allowing for spaces in between—around a hard surface (i.e., ruler, pencil) and count the number of threads that fit within a 1-inch space. If the count is the same, the yarns are essentially the same size; and if there is a discrepancy, the higher count will indicate the thinner thread.

Table 1-2. Conversion to the Tex System

System	Yarn Size Base	Conversion Factor	
Cotton	840 yd./lb.	590.5	
Linen	300 yd./lb.	1,654.0	
Woolen			Divide by
cut	300 yd./lb.	1,654.0	yarn size
run	1,600 yd./lb.	4,960.0	number
Worsted	560 yd./lb.	885.8	
Denier	9000 m./gm.	0.1111	Multiply by yarn size number

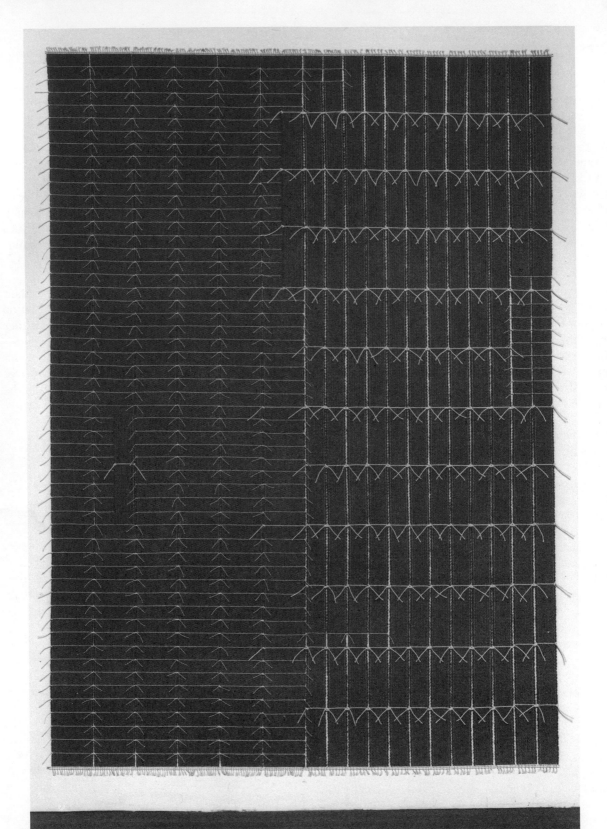

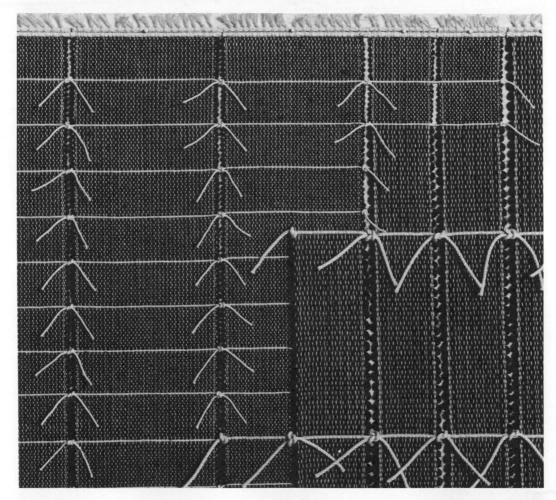

Blair Tate
Untitled/1982
linen, cotton rope
108" x 78" (274 x 198 cm.)

Inspired by the simultaneous order and deviation from pattern in African textiles, this untitled piece joins and confuses two clear halves. Each half consists of separately woven strips, joined by knotting, that are subdivided into identically proportioned but differently aligned and scaled woven areas. The change in scale is the result of using different-weight wefts both in the black woven areas and for the weft ropes. These different scales affect the warp/weft ratio, causing the same elements to appear as slightly different colors.

Untitled *is woven with a balanced weave warp density that, because of the relative inflexibility of the heavy weft, functions in an undulating warp-face manner. The size of the warp thread is very fine, with several threads grouped and treated as one. This resulting ribbon effect in the warp permits dense packing of the weft for an extremely tight weave construction. The fineness of the warp threads lends the fairly heavy weaving a sense of refinement. Because the natural color of the warp does not affect the whiteness of the weft ropes, these read as pure crisp elements. The warp color does, however, effectively tone the black weft, creating a color distinction between the integrated warp/weft color of the weaving and the pure black of the bulky weft when it is exposed at the edges of each strip. (Photographs: Stanley Rowin, Boston)*

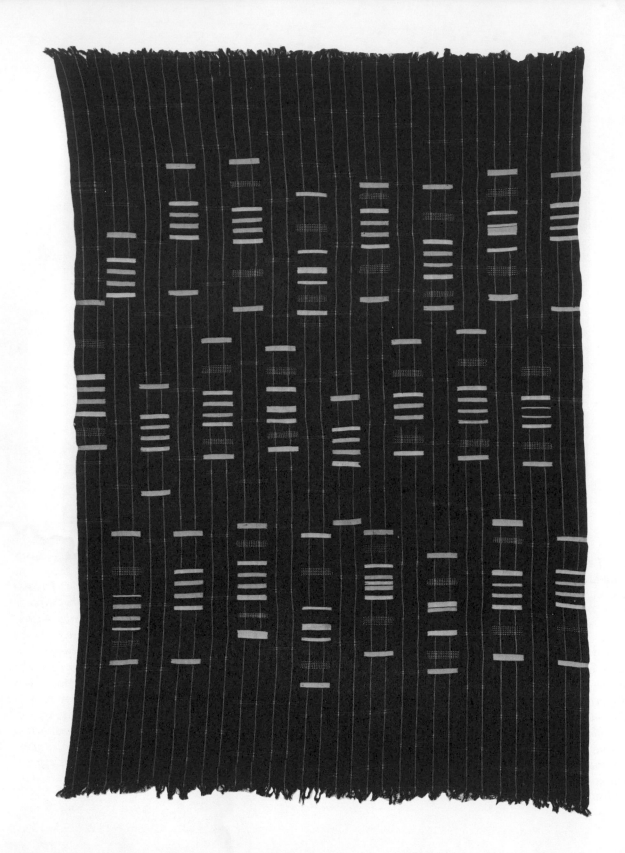

Ghana: Ashanti
Men's Weave: Kente Cloth/*early to mid-20th*
  century
cotton
96" x 60" (244 x 152 cm.)

This kente cloth is composed from separately woven warp-face strips into which bold weft-face horizontal bands have been intermittently introduced. These bands break up the monotony of the weave to produce unpredictable compositional variety.

The strip format lends itself to formal rearrangement before the strips are sewn together to form the broader cloth. The even spacing of the vertical warp stripes within each strip provides the whole cloth with a unified visual field while enabling maximum flexibility in each strip's orientation and relative location. A consistent woven line horizontally frames the work by running along each strip's top and bottom edge. Only the location of the horizontal weft bands varies from strip to strip. These bands can be either lined up, alternated to form a checker pattern, or charmingly mismatched, as they are here. (Photographs courtesy The American Museum of Natural History, New York)

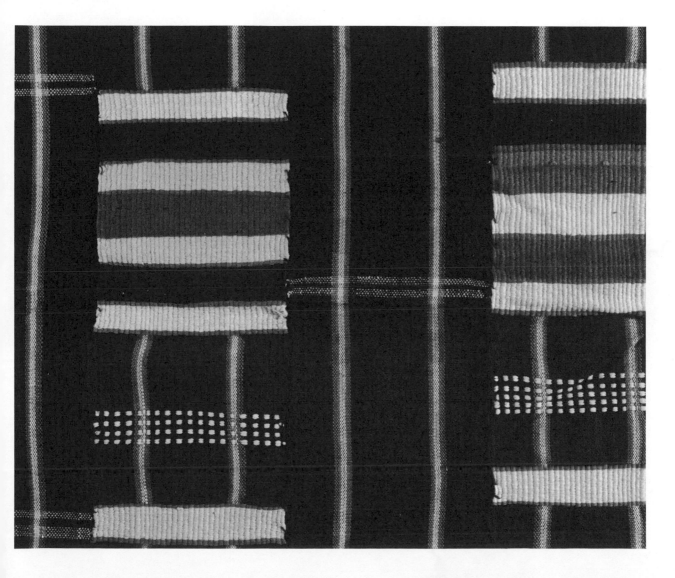

2 Density/Weave Mechanics

Density—the sett of the warp measured in number of threads per inch—is the most basic and perhaps most influential warp decision a weaver must make. Warp density governs the visual effect of the weave construction for the whole of the weaving.

Once established, warp density generally remains constant. It can be intentionally varied, but prefiguring is essential. Additions to the warp are extremely difficult to make because of the tension required if the warp is to function properly. Division of warp threads into layers, or deletion, is simpler but must be carefully planned in coordination with the threading pattern. Warp thread elimination, depending on quantity, can have an adverse effect on subsequent warp tension.

The density of the warp is determined in anticipation of its relationship to the weft. Its designation traditionally falls under three main categories, each descriptive of the essential warp/weft ratio: Warp-face indicates a predominance of warp; weft-face, a predominance of weft; balanced weave defines either the midpoint where there is an equal relationship between the two elements or is used in a more general sense to refer to any weaving in which both warp and weft are visible. For the purposes of this discussion, more specific, functionally descriptive terminology will be used: In *warp-face,* only the warp is visible; in *warp-face balanced,* the warp is more visually prevalent than the weft (although it still functions in a pure warp-face manner); *balanced weave* is used to describe weaving with an equal presence of warp and weft; *weft-face balanced* connotes a partially visible warp that is functionally encased by the weft (i.e., a warp that in action simulates the warp in a weft-face weave); and only the weft shows in *weft-face* weaving.

To figure the density for any of the different weave types, you must first figure the warp density of a balanced weave because it is the middle ground in the relationship between warp and weft. The simplest method for doing this is to firmly and uniformly wrap the proposed warp yarn around a smooth, hard surface in such a way that an equal amount of yarn and space is visible. Counting the yarns that fit within a 1-inch space gives the number for a balanced weave density.

Increasing or decreasing the number of warp yarns per inch from this balanced weave base number will change the weave type. It is generally thought that doubling the base will give the density for a warp-face weave and halving will give the density for weft-face. In actuality, for the absolute determination of warp-face density, this rule is not entirely accurate. Doubling determines the minimum quantity necessary for a pure warp-face weave and is more likely to create a warp-face balance. Pure warp-face generally requires a further increase. An exact formula cannot be set forth since scale of the yarn and choice of reed size are major, influencing variables—underscoring the advisability of weaving samples.

It is important to realize when figuring the warp density for each weave type that the number of threads per inch is not fixed. Even when given a specific yarn, weft choice and weave mechanics will have more influence than the simple quantity of threads does.

Let us assume, for the moment, a plain weave construction. Paired with different wefts, a 10/2 linen set at a density of 16 threads per inch could be party to most of the weave types. If paired with a sewing-thread-size flexible weft, the weave could be weft-face. With a slightly heavier and/or stiffer weft, a weft-face balance would be possible. Pairing with a yarn similar to its own size could produce a balanced weave, and use of a heavy weft would shift the ratio toward warp-face balanced. The only weave type it could not be is the extreme of warp-face because grouping 16 of this size thread within an inch space would not force the threads together enough to enable complete coverage of the weft, regardless of its size.

The five types of weave discussed here and below are separated in order to describe the inherent functioning and visual implications specific to each. An understanding of these distinctions will enable choices that correspond with and enhance whatever visual effect is desired.

Rather than begin at the customary beginning, with an examination of balanced weave, I have chosen to focus first on the action of the warp in warp-face weaving. Here, by virtue of sheer magnitude, the overriding effect of the warp is most clear. With warp reduction, and corresponding weft increase, the warp's fundamental influence becomes more subtle. It is my hope that understanding the warp in its most dominant role will facilitate recognition of its impact in all the other weaves.

WARP-FACE ›WARP-FACE BALANCED

Functionally, there is little difference in the warp's dominant role between warp-face and warp-face balanced weaving. In color, texture, and action, the warp unquestionably rules. In warp-face, the weft is entirely passive, and in warp-face balanced, it is slightly more assertive and thus marginally interactive.

Warp-Face

Warp-face density is extreme, and, as a result, the warp completely covers the weft (Fig. 2-1). The weave mechanics responsible for this are typically plain weave, or tabby, with alternate threads assigned to opposing sheds. Upon separation into these sheds, adjacent yarns shift position slightly and, in essence, stack themselves vertically. Two seemingly solid warp layers are formed, and the weft is placed between them. When the shed is switched behind the weft, that crossing completes the weft's encasement.

The warp actively surrounds the weft and molds itself following the weft's contour. In cross section, the warp undulates like a sine curve, and the weft runs a virtually straight path between the selvedges. Ac-

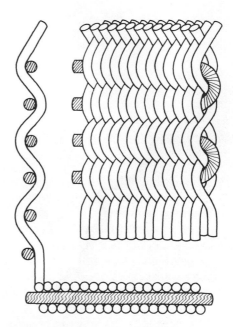

2-1. Warp-face weave

Warren Seelig
Grosgrain Roll/*1980*
cotton
4" x 6" x 3" (11 x 16 x 8 cm.)
Collection: Helen Drutt, Philadelphia

In Grosgrain Roll, a miniature, two tightly wound bolt lengths of identical, ribbed (grosgrain) fabric flank a horizontal stretch of inversely colored cloth. The inter-connection of these rolls increases awareness of their creation—their rolling together at some point—and tempts the mind with speculative revision of their size and distance apart. One's attention vacillates between the cylindrical rolls and ground level fabric, and move-ment is implied.

The cloth, by itself, is visually commanding and in-vites closer inspection. Its precisely woven warp-face construction is logarithmically graphed with narrow warp stripes defining the verticals and equally narrow weft ribs producing horizontals. The horizontal stripes are a consequence of alternately colored warp yarns and alternating thin and thick weft rows.

The density of the warp reduces the weft to its profile and renders its color invisible, except at the extreme edges. Here its exposure is used to balance the compo-sitional disparity between the fabric's selvedges. The broad band (on the left side of the strip) is faintly echoed by the minimal edge formed by the escaping weft (on the right). The color of the rolls' vertical surfaces (on both sides) is thus made uniform. (Photograph courtesy Hadler/Rodriguez Gallery, New York) cordingly, much of the warp's length, and almost none of the weft's, is absorbed by the weaving process. Warp length calculations must therefore be increased to allow for this expected take-up in the length. As a general rule, an increase of 25 percent should be sufficient. (To figure total warp length, see Appendix B.)

Because only the weft's profile is visible in the body of the weaving, the woven structure appears as a horizontal rib. Variations in weft dimension affect the rhythm of that rib. If warp yarns forming opposing sheds are each given a different color, then horizontal stripes will be produced. This striping accentuates the textural ribbing and makes it graphic.

The colors of both warp (in the body) and weft (at the edges) are seen purely and separately; there is no visual blending and mutual softening. The potential monotony of seeing either solid warp color or pure color stripes in the body of the weaving can be relieved by introducing either space-dyed (see *Tyla's Blanket*) or hand-painted warp threads prior to weaving. The weft color is glimpsed only briefly at the weaving's edge, where it escapes from one shed in order to disappear into another. Weft that is the same color as the warp appears as a slight, repeating, textural incident. Finely scaled weft is barely visible. But if the weft is of a different color or is texturally exaggerated, it punctuates the edge.

Double wefting is a weaving technique in which a weft coming from both sides of the weaving is simultaneously inserted in each row. In that case, rather than appearing and disappearing on alternate sides, the weft appears continuously on both. This method offers a clean finish by unifying the edge.

Strength of a fabric generally runs in the same direction as the warp, the warp yarns being relatively strong and continuous. This direction in a textile is known as the *lengthwise grain*. Because of the predominance of warp in warp-face weaving, the strength of the lengthwise grain is increased. The concentration of threads causes the fabric to be heavy and substantial. With less breathing room in the construction, there is less fluidity and drape. Because the weft's course is straight, there is little natural cross-grain pliability and, consequently, this direction is relatively stiff. The juncture between weft rows is seamlike and functions like a hinge, thus permitting flex along the horizontal axis.

For all these reasons, binding materials—straps, beltings, and ribbons—traditionally have been warp-face constructions. The warp makes them strong, their narrowness makes them tyable, and they bend well cross-grain so that they can be easily wrapped around three-dimensional forms. Their use of materials and method is economical in achieving maximum effect.

Furthermore, narrow warp-face weaving is far easier to weave than wider widths are. In the latter, sheer abundance of warp increases the difficulty of operating the loom. The density of the threads causes crowding in the heddles; the almond-shaped heddle eyes tend to catch on each other, hampering, if not rendering impossible, the switching of the sheds. Fibrous or sticky yarns further complicate matters as the threads are then also grabbing each other. This basic problem can be reduced by spreading the threads across multiple harnesses—for example, using eight rather than four—to reduce the proximity of heddles within each harness. But warp tension required during the weaving process still places physical limits on the operation of the harnesses. The threads under tension will try to remain straight and keep all the harnesses in alignment. The more threads per harness, the more weight must be applied to counter the tension and forcibly change the harness's position. With narrower widths, on the other hand, the weight of each harness frame assists the harness-changing action. Increasing the weaving width increases the weight necessary for raising or lowering the harnesses. Generally, the heavier the loom, the less this is a problem—but for every loom and/or weaver, there is a definite limit.

Warp-face weaving, when the loom is cooperating, is generally quick. More time is required in warp preparation but less in actual weaving. The seamlike shed crossings that flank every weft row physically contribute to the woven length. Hence fewer picks are necessary to advance the weaving.

VARIATIONS AFFECTING WARP-FACE DENSITY
Through functional regrouping of the warp threads, pure warp-face weaving can be turned into pure weft-

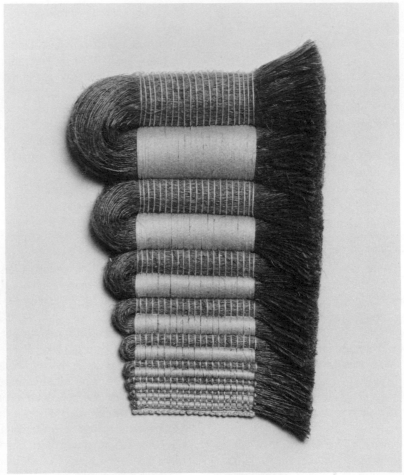

Blair Tate
Shadow Rows/*1980*
cotton, linen
7½" x 5" x 1½" (19 x 13 x 4 cm.)
Collection: Deborah Daw, Cambridge, Massachusetts

In the most basic sense, the process of weaving involves the line-by-line accumulation of wefts within the warp's controlling framework. The clear order associated with simple numerical progressions parallels this systematic growth in a weaving. In the miniature, Shadow Rows, number and thread are equated such that the form results from the translation of a numerical progression into counted weft threads physically compressed within each row.

The progression used is repeated doubling, in which the sum of two continuous weft rows equals the number of yarns needed for the next set. The repeated rows are distinguished by alternating warp densities. The pure warp-face density completely encases the weft, while the reduced density clearly exposes it. Each pair of weft rows increases the vertical growth of the fabric, while dimensional expansion occurs from pair to pair. The tight, logical consistency gives the piece a sense of balance despite its asymmetrical profile. Because of the doubling progression, the weft thread quantities rapidly become enormous. The dense compaction of these threads in each row gives the piece a physical presence beyond its actual size. (Photograph: Stanley Rowin, Boston) face weaving (see Weft-Face Density in this chapter). To make this possible, the warp density is reduced by treating several adjacent threads as if they were one. In cross section, that "single" entity is flat and broad, almost tapelike. In order to encase it to create weft-face weaving, only very pliable, relatively small-scale weft yarns can be used. During the weaving process, these yarns are given a lot of extra length to enable them to undulate around the warp groups. Their small scale takes maximum advantage of the minute space between groups and allows sequential rows to be packed down.

A similar weft-face effect can be achieved by simply not allowing the weft to interact with every warp thread. There can be a second, or supplementary, weft floating across the surface and tying into the warp at regular or irregular intervals. This weft could be considered a brocade.

The visual difference between these two wefting methods is in the sense of depth and reversibility. In the first method (see *Men's Weave: Kente Cloth*), both warp-face and weft-face lie in the same plane. All threads are either actively encasing or being passively encased; hence the cloth is reversible. Alternation in yarn color would cause a reversal in image, but both sides would be texturally the same. With weft brocading (see *Swag*) the weft projects forward of the warp-face plane on one side and makes no impression on the other. This inequality produces definitive front and back faces. On the front, the raised weft can be seen in relief against the warp-face ground, thus establishing a subtle hierarchy of figure/ground.

The idea of a secondary weft can be taken further. Instead of being intermittently tacked into the woven cloth, it can be fully interwoven. When the warp is divided into two layers to form the opposing shed, each layer can be subdivided to encase its own, separate weft; this principle can be extended to create three or more layers. With reduction in warp density, each layer will shift toward balanced and weft-face.

With the formation of woven layers, a broad range of textural options becomes possible. In balanced weave layers (see Balanced Weave in this chapter), each has the potential to be flatter—more uniform in cross-sectional analysis—and, in effect, more planar.

Because of the direct alignment of these woven planes, they have cumulative bulk, which causes them to project forward of the undulating, texturally ribbed, warp-face weaving. The degree of planar projection increases with either an increase in the number of layers, use of heavier weft, or shift in each layer's weave type towards weft-face (where each layer is by nature heavier).

The separate layers can simply rest next to each other like stacked sheets of paper, or they can be pulled apart, accentuating the negative space between or filling it with some sort of stuffing (see *Vertical Shield #2*). With the latter, the character of the stuffing has a pronounced visual effect: The parallel layered bands can be tightly filled with a relatively soft stuffing to give the effect of a much grosser scale warp-face rib. Insertion of flat rigid structures would stiffen the cloth like battens or stays in a sail; and shaped infrastructures give the cloth a very different form from its original, flat-woven shape.

With the use of pick-up techniques, two (or more) layers can be made to switch their relative (above/below) positions at any point during the weaving. If the same color warp yarns are assigned to both layers, this crossover will produce textural quiltlike seaming. With contrasting colors, blocky graphic imagery is possible.

Warp-Face Balanced

Reverting back to a plain weave construction and only slightly reducing the quantity of warp threads from warp-face density will produce warp-face balanced weaves. In these, the warp still basically envelops the weft, hence the same percentage of warp length increase is necessary for weaving. (To calculate the total warp length, see Appendix B.) The primary texture remains as it was in warp-face—horizontal ribs—but the weft becomes visible throughout the body of the fabric. The colors of both warp and weft begin to be seen together, affecting each other in a visual blend. Warp color still predominates, but it is toned by the weft.

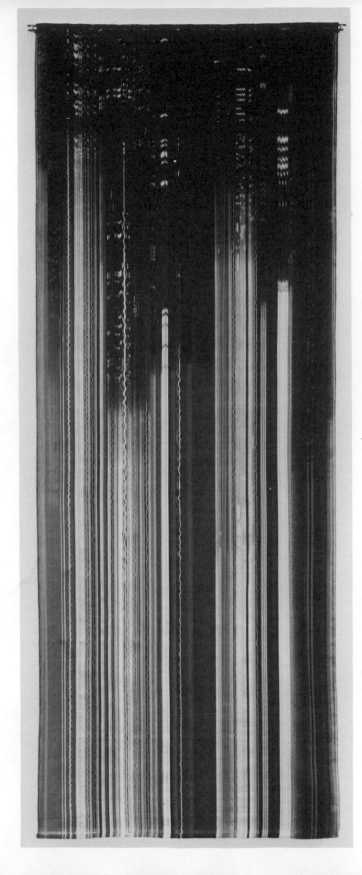

Jayn Thomas
Wing Light/*1983*
cotton
94" x 41" (239 x 104 cm.)
Collection: First National Bank of Boston

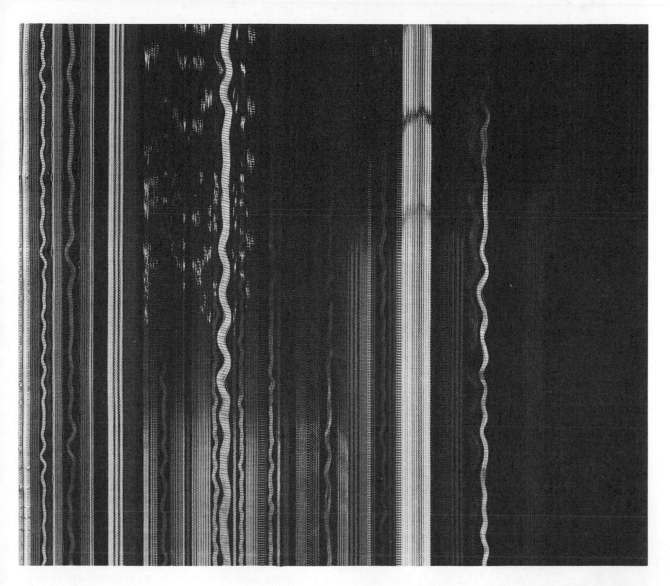

Wing Light *explores the uneven transition between pure color and flickering shadow. The texturally striped fabric, resulting from broad and narrow reed marks, seems to gradually evolve. Its color and texture are initially disguised by the butterflylike shimmer and vibration of the horizontally ikatted warp bands. As the black overdye fades out, the grayed, muted colors gather intensity, and their texture becomes steadily clearer until the warp emerges as a brightly colored, rhythmic series of stripes. The loose, weft-encased, unwoven warps ripple down the surface, relieving the strict verticality of what would otherwise be simply beautiful, but not unfamiliar, striped cloth.*

The weave in Wing Light *is essentially a finely scaled warp-face balance with the weft uniformly spaced by the dense warp. The sewing thread size of the elements causes the fabric to be extremely thin and delicate, giving it a gossamer character. The spaced weft enables the cloth to be intermittently transparent. This transparency contributes to the ephemeral, shadowy quality of the tapestry's upper half. (Photographs: David Caras, Boston)*

In warp-face balanced weaves, the amount of weft visibility is only partly due to warp quantity; the choice of reed size plays perhaps the more significant role in determining the visual texture of the weave. Reeds available for handweaving range in densities of from 4 to 30 dents (or spaces) per inch, with the thickness of the wire used to create these spaces steadily reducing as the number of spaces increases. The dividing wires can be likened to fence uprights that cast parallel "shadows," known as *reed marks,* on the woven cloth. These shadows are simply the absence of warp threads, and it is because of their existence that the weft can be seen (Fig. 2-2).

With strong, finely scaled, dimensionally smooth warp threads, you can choose to weave using any density reed, whereas slightly weaker, thicker, or more textural yarns can be threaded only through the larger spaces in the reeds with lower densities. Single and uniform *sleying* (drawing of the warp threads through the slots in the reed) in a high-density, thinner wire reed produces minimal shadows on the cloth. The regular alternation of thread and shadow is so natural that it is hardly noticeable; it certainly poses no challenge to the warp's ability to visually overpower and neutralize the weft. With use of lower-density, heavier wire reeds, the weft begins to become more prominent. Grouping (or multiple sleying) of the warp threads through these fewer, broader spaces with larger divisions between them causes the warp to become rhythmically, vertically striped. The weft color, as a result, is exposed in more concentrated amounts. Uneven sleying, with spaces left vacant, will alter the rhythm of the warp striping to reveal even more of the weft. (For warp density/reed density pattern distributions, see Appendix C.)

When the reed marks are pronounced, use of a thin weft will cause the reed mark stripe to be almost transparent. The warp's encasement automatically spaces the weft within the weft rows, creating an effect that is gauzelike because the separated weft permits easy passage of light. With use of a relatively thick weft, the vertical warp striping and the horizontal rib texture will create a balanced weave appearance, despite the weave mechanics to the contrary.

BALANCED WEAVE

In balanced weaving, equal amounts of warp and weft are exposed (Fig. 2-3). Both elements interact, engaging in a continuous dance of control and response, assertion and submission. Neither dominates visually—the texture and color of both blend equally. Examined in cross section, both warp and weft can be seen continually shifting their positions in deference to each other. They share the same basic plane: The ups and downs are barely pronounced and there is no alternate swelling (to accommodate weft) and pinching (line of shed change). Because the weft is now active, the warp's undulation is reduced, and, consequently, absorption of the warp's length in balanced weaving is considerably lower than in warp-face weaving. In warp length calculations, generally only a 10 percent increase is necessary. (To figure total warp length, see Appendix B.)

The equal distribution of threads between both elements places a much lower ceiling on the total number of threads possible within a square inch. This lower density gives breathing room to the construction.

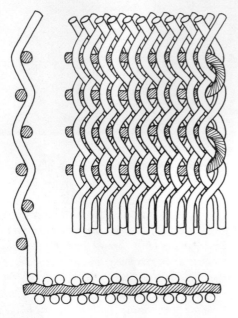

2-2. Warp-face balanced weave (showing reed marks)

Consequently, the weave is thinner, lighter, and—if not countered by choice of a naturally rigid material, such as wire or paper—more flexible than any of the other weave types. Because the warp/weft density is equal, there is no directional emphasis in the woven grid. As a result, lengthwise and crosswise grains are equally pliable and the fabric's ability to drape in any direction becomes not only possible but probable. Balanced weave is therefore traditionally the weave type used in cloth and clothing.

With separate but equal visibility of both elements, true color blending (as opposed to toning) is possible. Extreme value differences cause visual vibration between the two elements, which activates the surface. If either the scale of the yarn is decreased or the viewing distance increased, a visual fusion of the two colors takes place. The new color produced by the impressionistic synthesis is necessarily complex because it is not a single color. It retains vibrancy and is not flat.

Because it is so basic and adaptable, balanced weave is the most common and logical first choice for learning about weaving. In balanced weave, warp and weft must share the limelight. As opposing elements, their fight for visual supremacy is most keen because in all respects they are equally matched. Yet despite this equivalence, there is a crucial difference between them: The warp is a constant, affecting the whole of the weaving, while the weft is an independent variable, whose size, color, and texture can be changed at any point.

Because balanced weave does not have the directionality or specific textural effects inherent in the other weave types, it can be considered more neutral. As such, it serves well as a ground for supplementary pattern elements, which can be, and often are, used together in the same work.

Supplementary Warp

A supplementary warp, or *warp brocade,* is essentially nonstructural (Fig. 2-4). It is incorporated into the weaving for purely visual reasons and its appearance is generally that of vertical floats—parallel lines of threads that rest on the surface of the underlying woven web. Supplementary warp can be either thin or lush, sporadic or abundant, but whichever, it clearly

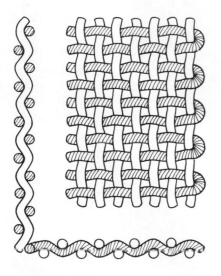

2-3. Balanced weave

2-4. Balanced weave with supplementary warp floats

Virginia Davis
Kasureru 8/1981
double ikat silk
48" x 36 " (122 x 91 cm.)

In Kasureru 8, *the image results from color shifts within the individual threads, rather than from the introduction of separate, different-colored yarns, as in traditional tapestry. The unbroken plain weave is in a balanced construction that allows for maximum visual interaction between warp and weft.*

Kasureru *is Japanese for the cloudy appearance of the* end of a brush stroke. Its meaning perfectly describes the effect of ikat, where color appears and disappears along each thread's length, sharply defining the thread's profile, while feathering at the boundaries between dyed and undyed sections. The softened transition between different-colored segments suggests movement in each individual line of yarn. The lines visually dissolve, rather than abruptly stopping.*

The forms defined in Kasureru 8 *coalesce from an accumulation of ikat-activated lines. Although the shapes are roughly rectangular, their furtive edges overcome the static weight of pure geometry. (Photographs: Virginia Davis, New York)*

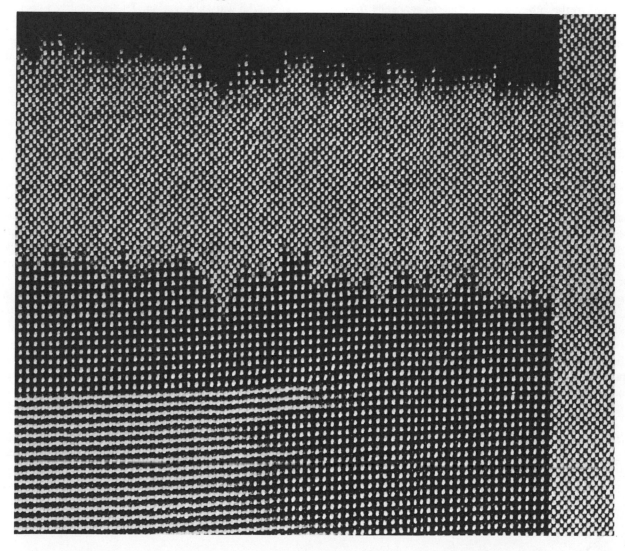

distinguishes itself from the body of the weaving. Its threads project forward of the woven surface and are pure elements, uncompromised by interaction with other threads. The aesthetic contribution of supplementary warp can vary from providing textural variety to being an additional, almost decorative element, to becoming visually dominant and providing the central imagery for the work.

The decision to include a supplementary warp and the determination of its character must be made more or less concurrently with the other, primary/structural warp preparations. Because it is a type of warp, it is subject to the standard warp requirements. Its position relative to the other warp threads is generally fixed, but its emergence and disappearance are optional—it can be brought to the surface at the weaver's whim.

Because a supplementary warp is not actually woven, its tension often becomes slack in relation to that of the primary warp threads. The length of the structural warp is being absorbed and effectively reduced because of its undulation in deference to the weft. The supplementary warp length, on the other hand, is unaffected by weft interaction and, by comparison, appears to grow and lose tension.

Tensioning the supplementary warp independently by beaming it onto a second warp beam can help to offset this growth. Uniform tension, however, can only be maintained in instances where the full supplementary warp is acting in unison. The effectiveness of the second warp beam is greatly reduced wherever use or disuse of the supplementary warp threads varies considerably.

Without consistent tension to enforce strict verticality, the supplementary warp threads tend to sway across the surface of the weaving. This effect further contrasts the two warp elements—the nonwoven and the woven—and can be used to expose and accentuate the basic quality of unmanipulated yarns.

Supplementary Weft

Supplementary weft, also known as *secondary* or *pattern weft* or *weft brocade,* is also nonstructural. It is basically the horizontal equivalent to the vertical supplementary warp, but in action it is a far freer agent. Supplementary weft is wholly independent of loom control and suffers no warp requirement restrictions. Its placement need not be predetermined; its length is fully controllable by the weaver; and its elements do not even have to be parallel to one another. Generally, but not always, a supplementary weft is heavier than its corresponding woven ground weft and visually obscures it.

However, the use of supplementary weft is not always clear sailing; its introduction can pose problems for warp tension. Wherever the floating weft brocade feeds back into the woven web, its added bulk increases the warp absorption. The cumulative effect of erratic tie-ins can virtually rob the warp of its original uniform tension. Because this affects the basic woven ground, it creates a potentially more serious situation than variable supplementary warp tension does. Inconsistencies can be countered but only through considerable effort—groups of threads or, if necessary, each thread can be separately tensioned by individual stuffing (see chapter 6, Tension Problems).

Selvedge Treatments

The general thinness of balanced weaving can be reinforced at its edge by special handling of the warp. This handling, known as a selvedge treatment, can be used to refocus attention to the weaving's edge. The selvedge can frame the work and keep the viewer's eye from wandering off the woven page.

Selvedge treatments (Fig. 2-5) can be executed in a number of ways. The most standard method is to double the quantity of threads at the selvedge, thus introducing a warp-face density at the woven edge (*A* in the figure). This method economically counters some of the difficulties inherent in balanced weaving. First of all, with the continual entry and escape of weft threads in subsequent rows, there is an almost unavoidable increase in manipulation of the weaving's edge. The edge yarns bear the brunt of the escaping weft's distorting pull whenever the weft is dragged across them and placed to rest on top of the finished cloth. Yarns that by their nature can grow more easily

A   Double Density Selvedge

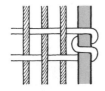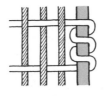

B   Additional Cord Selvedges

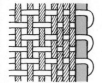

C   Double Density and Additional Cord Selvedges Combined

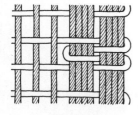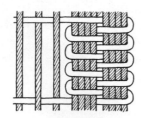

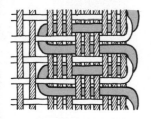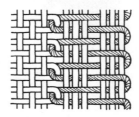

D   Woven Selvedges

2-5. Selvedge treatments

than they can shrink (such as linen and mercerized cotton) suffer visibly from this. As they stretch, they lose tension and vitality. No longer functioning in an equal capacity with the weft, these edge threads will tend to wander, and weave erratically. Warp-face density works in opposition to this growth. Because the extreme undulation of the warp threads increases warp absorption, it counters the appearance of growth and sagging: Instead, the warp "shrinks" and tightens.

Secondly, warp-face construction regularly spaces the weft, facilitating the weaving of a consistent number of weft picks per inch. And finally, increased concentration of threads thickens the edge.

This method is usually used in conjunction with either a tabby or basket weave (two threads acting as one, but otherwise similar to plain weave) construction. The grouped threads of the basket weave will enable the weft threads in the body of the fabric to be more closely packed. The direct alternation of shed (in either) gives consistency to the woven edge.

A second method, more commonly used in weft-face weaving, but applicable to balanced, involves the addition of a strong supplemental yarn on each side (*B* in Fig. 2-5). This yarn is usually thicker than the standard warp thread and is not beamed along with the rest of the warp. Instead, it is individually weighted and hung off the back of the loom. These supplemental yarns are generally not threaded and are manually caught by passing the weft alternately under and over them or around them. Because they are tensioned separately from the warp, they are immune to the usual warp strains. They function as self-adjusting edge guides and provide a clean finish, which is particularly helpful when a pattern threading/treadling prevents alternate rows of the weaving from evenly offsetting each other (as in a twill weave).

Sometimes a combination of these two methods is used (*C* in Fig. 2-5). Although this might seem redundant, its visual effect is striking. In the balanced weave center of the cloth, warp and weft are seen together, blending in equal amounts. Passing into the doubled warp-face density selvedge, the weft color is wholly or partially obscured. The weft then emerges purely as it wraps around the edge guide. The selvedge

finish
edges
selvage
4 mead
m final
ley

loore
cord)

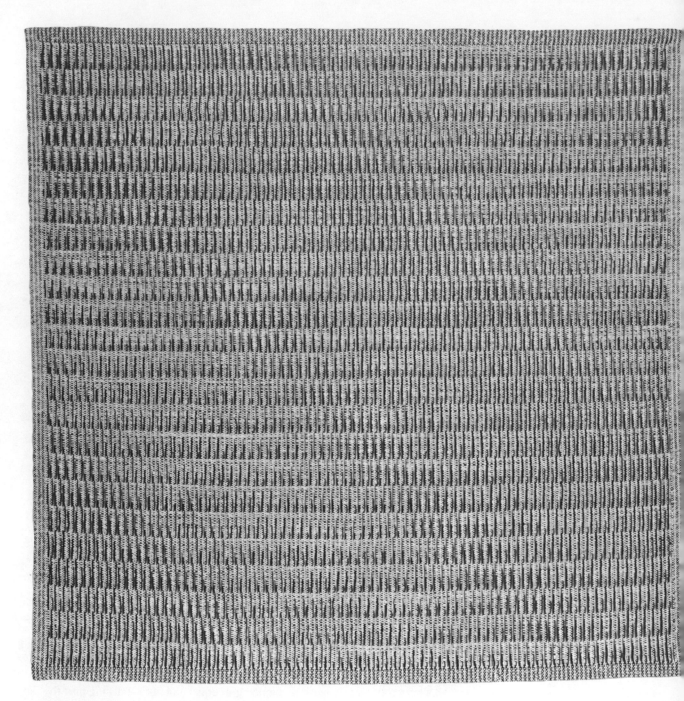

Margot Rolf
Starting from 4-Colors VII-13/*1977*
linen
79" x 79" (200 x 200 cm.)

In Starting from 4-Colors VII-13, *a subtle color field is created by the impressionistic blend of brocaded warp elements. These are arranged in horizontal bands of vertical warp lines, reminiscent of rhythmic rows of type-characters with their even spacing and fluctuating heights.*

The weave is made up of consistently sequenced red, yellow, green, and blue linen warp yarns partially encased by white linen weft. The bold color warp lines stand out, both physically and graphically, from the diffused texture of the weft-face balanced ground weave. The lines appear at first to be a complex, exceedingly versatile brocade. But on closer scrutiny, they reveal themselves to be part of the structural warp and merely exempted from the weave at will. The warp's minimal interaction with the weft, and consequent lack of absorption in the weave, enables the exposed warp threads to maintain their strict, tensioned verticality.

The work is visually framed by the weaving of heavy tubular selvedges on each side and folded (hence, two layer) ground cloth on both the top and bottom edges. Both of these weaves condense all the warp/weft ingredients that constitute the tapestry into a clear, simple plane. The pale color of these borders, in which the pure colored warp is washed by the white weft, has a bleaching effect on the work, reinforcing its atmospheric quality. (Photographs: Studio 68, Amsterdam, whole view; and Jeffrey Schiff, Boston, detail)

Nancy Guay
Sarahan I/*1977*
linen, cotton, silk, rayon, metallics, saran,
polypropylene
42" x 60" (107 x 152 cm.)

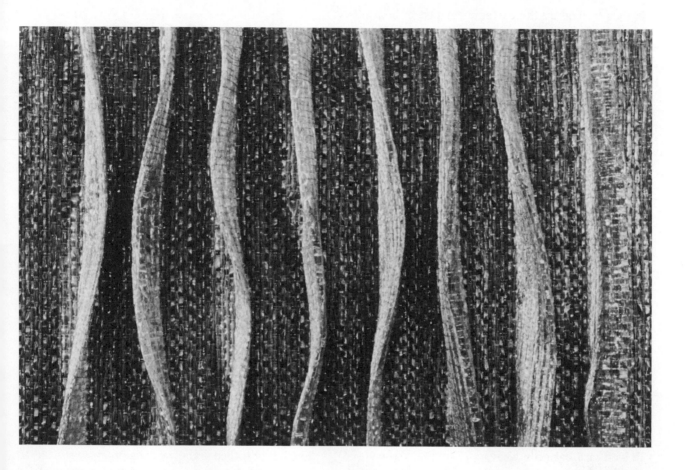

Sarahan I *is made of transparent, translucent, and se-mireflective materials that shimmer and change color in response to ambient light. Pleats are used as a means to create and isolate separate woven surfaces. The pleats are projected forward in strong, pliable planes so that they will function both graphically and sculpturally. If the work is viewed frontally, the crisp undulating profile of each pleat stands out against the denser and more distant ground. Viewed from the side, controlled variations in the pleats' color and translucency cause light to dance across the tapestry field.*

The weave structure and choice of weft yarn together permit the penetration of light through two layers of weaving in the pleats. The warp is widely spaced, with a weft-face balanced density, and is used in conjunction with a flat, broad, light-transmitting weft. The distance between warps is insufficient to allow the ribbonlike weft to pack down in a weft-face weave, yet is not so close that alone it would cause opacity. The warp sett keeps the weft rows pure and separated from one another, as if stacked. This allows the weave to be dimensionally thin and yet structurally tight and firm. In contrast, the ground weave texture is solid and heavy, with more warp threads incorporated and several weft yarns compressed in each row. (Photographs: Greg Heins, Boston) is thus formed by the extreme contrast of both elements.

Woven selvedges, conceptually related to the wrapped-edge cord, are shown in *D* in Fig. 2-5. These involve increased activity by the weft and follow weft-face principles. Groups of warp threads are treated as a single, encasable entity (reminiscent of Kente cloth). Depending on the scale of the weft, the weaving will be either weft-face balanced or pure weft-face. In either case, the edge will be thicker and the weft will be automatically spaced in the body of the fabric. However, the warp absorption will be correspondingly reduced—indicating the advisability of separately tensioning these selvedge warp threads.

WEFT-FACE BALANCED → WEFT-FACE

In weavings that are either weft-face balanced or weft-face, the weft predominates by essentially encapsulating the warp. In weft-face balanced, coverage is partial and warp interaction is slight; in weft-face, there is total coverage of the virtually passive warp.

Weft-Face Balanced

In weft-face balanced weaving (Fig. 2-6), the weft is clearly superior, both visually and functionally, but it is not in full control. Its inability to completely obscure the warp can result from material choice, from handling, or from both. The weft can be too heavy, too broad, or too inflexible to take advantage of the space between warp threads in order to pack down around them. Insufficient weft length can offset a yarn's inherent flexibility and prevent firm packing, as can very gentle beating.

Conversely, the warp can be too closely spaced to permit the weft to fully undulate about it. Where several warp threads act together, becoming cross-sectionally broad and flat (as in Kente cloth), the weight and length of the weft will determine its amount of coverage. For the warp to keep its interaction with

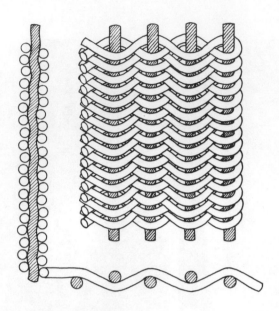

2-6. Weft-face balanced weave

the weft at a minimum, as required for weft-face weaving, warp tension must be both taut and uniform. Relaxation in tension will encourage interaction and prevent full weft-face coverage, even if all the other elements and conditions would indicate it.

Because of the warp's relative passivity, little of its length is absorbed in the weaving process, and the 10 percent increase over desired finished length used for determining balanced weave warp length may be excessive. The degree of weft coverage can be determined by weaving samples, and this should be used as the indicator for determining a more accurate percentage increase. If coverage is almost complete, then 5 percent should be sufficient. However, if actual coverage is variable, 10 percent should be used. (To calculate total warp length, see Appendix B.)

The increased quantity of weft used in this weave increases the total number of threads per square inch and makes the fabric heavier. The fabric also becomes firmer, losing the drapability of balanced weave.

Since the weft affords only brief glimpses of the warp, weft color and texture are paramount. The warp's contribution is tonal and dimensional. Because of the visual diffusion, the vertical ribbing associated with weft-face weaves, although present, is less pronounced than in pure weft-face.

Weft-Face

In certain respects, weft-face is the equivalent of pure warp-face, but rotated 90° (Fig. 2-7). The weft color and texture are seen purely, with the warp color only appearing at the very beginning and end of the fabric. There is no visual blending between the two elements. The warp's presence is felt only skeletally, as the underlying structure supporting the weft. The weft envelops the warp, defining its profile by creating a vertical rib.

Here, all undulation is the province of the weft, and the weft's length is exaggerated accordingly. The warp is completely passive. Warp threads are actively manipulated by the harnesses to facilitate weaving, but there is no physical interaction with the weft. The warp operates under extreme tension, running a straight and parallel path from start to finish. None of the warp length is affected by the weaving process, so an increase beyond the loom loss factor is unnecessary. However, a precautionary 5 percent increase is advisable. (To calculate total warp length, see Appendix B.)

In weft-face, the weft density, or number of weft picks per vertical inch, is at an extreme high for whatever yarn is being used. For warp coverage to be complete, consecutive rows must exactly complement each other. The weave mechanics for this are either plain weave or a variation on plain weave known as rep, rib, or bound weave (in which two threads are being treated as one). In order for the weave to function properly, the scale of the weft yarn is limited: Two rows cannot compress together if the yarns of either row are too heavy or unequal in size. Since two rows must pack down to visually simulate a single line, the weaving process is considerably slower than in any other weave type.

The fabric resulting from all this weft compression

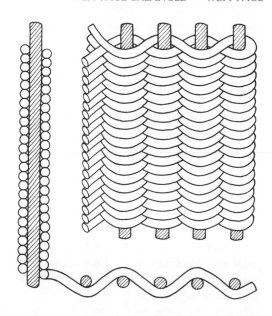

2-7. Weft-face weave

is dense and heavy, stiff rather than pliable. Weft-face weaving should be considered wherever strength and body are principal concerns. For this reason, it is standardly used in the creation of flat-woven rugs.

WEFT-FACE TAPESTRY

Because all attention is focused on the weft, weft-face weaving is also customary in traditional tapestry. The weft is the free element, unencumbered by loom constraints. It can be of any material—weak or strong, structured or not, textured or plain—and can be introduced or deleted at any point in the weaving. With free wefting and hand beating, weft rows do not have to be straight and parallel. The weaver is in full control. Any sort of imagery is possible, although roughly locked within the grid structure of weaving, and preplanning is optional—dramatic revisions can be made while the work is in progress.

Horizontal shapes tend to be both faster and easier to make, and crisper in appearance. With longer wefts, there is less work required within each row. Clear horizontal distinctions are easily made by inserting a different-colored weft. But potential confusion always exists within each row at the vertical boundaries between these wefts. Myriad techniques—interlocking, dove-tailing, sewing together of kilim slits—have been developed in an attempt to resolve this awkward juncture. For this reason, many finely scaled traditional tapestries with principally vertical images have been woven on their sides.

Basically, there are only two limitations in weft-face tapestry:

1. The roughly horizontal, linear development of the image makes change in the completed part of the tapestry exceedingly difficult. Once the weaving has progressed beyond an area, subsequent revision can be accomplished only by tedious removal and reworking. Since there are considerably more wefts per vertical inch, their removal is a major undertaking.

2. Scale and sett of the warp predetermine the sense of refinement or crudeness possible in the imagery. The options for visually changing the weft's length of line falls in the spaces between the warp threads.

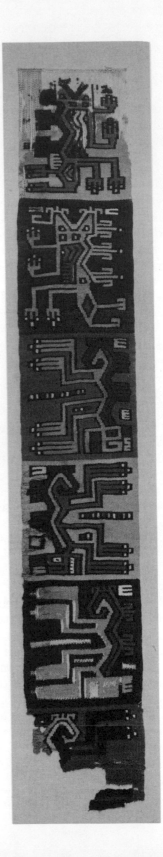

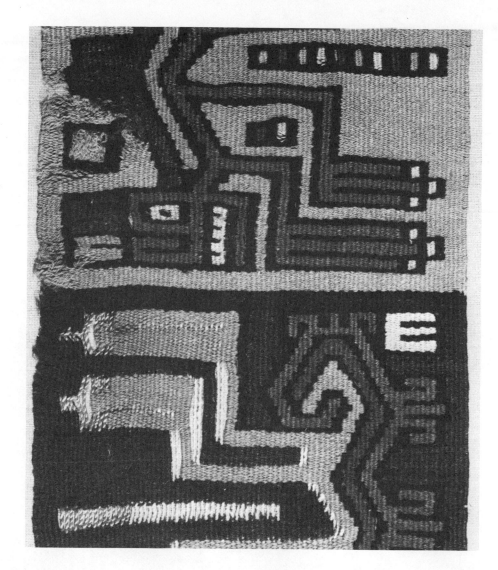

Peru: South Coast, Nasca
Six Stylized Animals/*Middle Horizon 500–900*
wool, cotton
35" x 5½" (89 x 14 cm.)
16.42, Ross Collection

The imagery in this weft-face woven Peruvian band plays within, but never attempts deviation from, the strong verticals and horizontals of the woven grid. Diagonal lines are formed by stepping, and all the vertical lines are created by the weft encasement of two adjacent warp yarns. The tapestry is in essence a series of tiny separate weavings with frequent joins.

The absence of warp in certain areas, and weft in others, boldly acclaims the fundamental, structural significance of the warp. Where the warp is missing (visible in the upper half of the detail), the remaining weft is texturally confused. The strong ribbing in evidence elsewhere is gone. Where the weft has disintegrated (in the detail's lower half), the warp is unaffected. It is pure and straight, and crisply records the form previously occupied by the weft. The surrounding geometry remains intact. The warp is exposed as the weaving's internal framework—as its essential spine. (Photographs courtesy Museum of Fine Arts, Boston)

Morocco: Zemmour
Rug/mid 20th century
wool
108" x 54" (274 x 137 cm.)

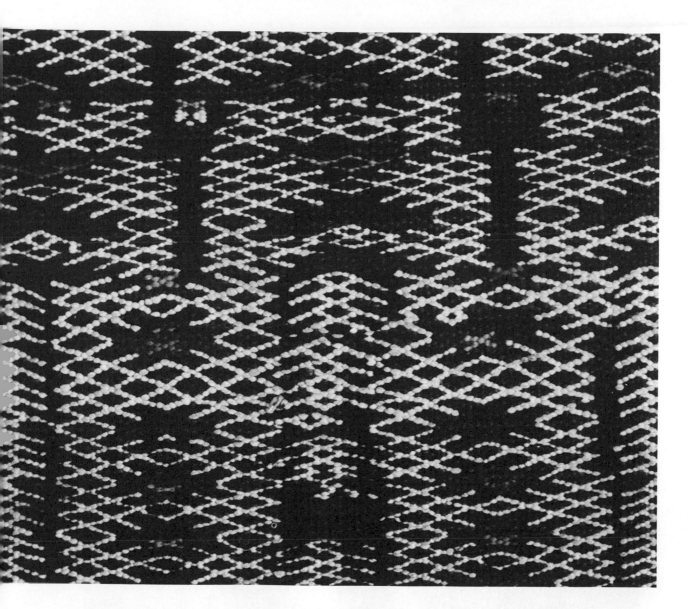

This weft-face woven contemporary Moroccan carpet, made by Berber weavers, sparkles with variety of detail. It is woven in what has been called "skip plain weave," in which the linear pattern is the result of weft substitutions that cover individual warp threads. Because of this, the sett of the warp very directly determines the pattern potential in the weaving.

The patterns are all created by uniform shifting of the white weft to cover the adjacent warp yarn in each successive row. Since this is done consistently, the angle of the diagonal line thus formed remains constant. Combining these simple diagonals permits the creation of seemingly endless varieties of geometric pattern. Of special interest is the complete avoidance of any vertical seams. As mentioned in the general text, special tapestry techniques are usually required to structurally resolve vertical junctures. Here, without physically interrupting the weave, strong vertical lines are created by implication—the patterns are simply stacked, with darker weft areas left in between. (Photographs: Stanley Rowin, Boston)

Lewis Knauss
View from the Excelsior/*1981*
hemp sewing twine, linen, paint
44" x 36" (112 x 91 cm.)

3 Finishing

View from the Excelsior *was inspired by the Middle Eastern string door curtains that simultaneously invite and forbid, offering the possibility of physical entry but denying visual penetration. The tapestry re-creates and expands upon this theme. A woven ground supports regularly released weft tendrils, which fall and accumulate, obscuring their origin. Gravity transforms these wefts into supplementary warp, and new warps are added. These are joined by knotting, thickened by braiding, and further diverted by subsequent additions. The once orderly whole becomes an inscrutable, textural field, and the underlying woven structure is completely lost. The image is developed more in its complex finishing than in its on-loom weaving. (Photograph: Lewis Knauss, Philadelphia)*

When the weaving is finished, the warp cannot be simply cut from the loom and left—the warp ends must be secured in some manner. The structural and visual integrity of the weaving depends upon this.

The possibilities for warp-end finishes are diverse and unlimited. Diagrams of some options follow. These are roughly divided into two groups: those that include the warp ends as fringe and those that visually eliminate them. The separate methods, and the specific ways in which they are used, carry with them very different implications.

Keeping the warp ends visible, either by inclusion of a fringe or by exposure as a broad or thin edge, accentuates the specificity of the woven article. The warp ends distinguish warp from weft and refer to the loom's role in manufacture. They can frame the work or soften the visual edge between the weaving and the wall, table, or floor. Fringe length can alter the sense of general shape and size and either enhance or distract from the woven portion of the work. The size and type of knot (if this is the technique used) and consequent grouping of fringe threads affect the sense of overall scale.

In contrast, a hemmed edge can seem cut from a longer length—in essence, cropped. If all four edges are hemmed, warp and weft may lose their identifiability. The closed finish can diminish one's sense of the size of the work, keeping its physical presence confined within its actual border. This may cause the weaving to relate more to two-dimensional painting and drawing than to three-dimensional sculpture.

The finish must also take into account the means of presentation. If the work is to hang vertically, either by direct attachment to the wall or through suspension away from it, this requirement must be engineered into the finish. The work might be hung from a single point or several points. Frequently, a broad edge might be tacked or secured with Velcro, or some method may be found for stiffening or rigidifying it. Stiffening could be achieved by using dense *horizontal clove hitches,* also called double half-hitches (Fig. 3-1); *twining* (see Fig. 3-3) with a naturally stiff material such as wire, heavy cord, or basketry reed; or repeating some of the fringeless edge finishes. Rigidifying involves the visible or concealed addition of some already stiff element, such as wire, rod, or batten. Scale and character of the element (if visible), as well as the hardware or cords necessary to secure the installation, are all equally important visual considerations. Ideally, the finishing method, or range of possibilities, should be determined before the start of the weaving in order to be adequately provided for.

WARP AS FRINGE

Treating warp ends as fringe is the most basic way in which to finish a work. Most methods begin by keeping the fringe as a straight, vertical element (Figs. 3-2, 3-3, 3-4).

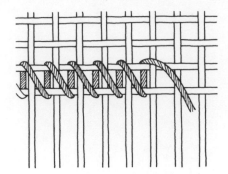

Overcasting

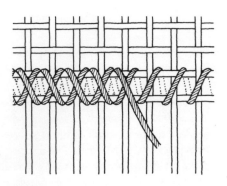

Cross-stitching

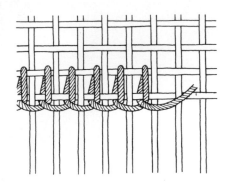

Blanket Stitching

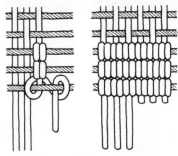

Horizontal Clove Hitches

3-1. Edge stiffening

3-2. Ungrouped fringes

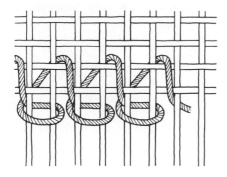

Hemstitching

Overhand Knot

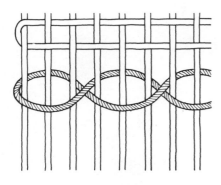

Twining

3-3. Barely grouped fringes

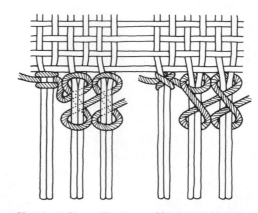

Vertical Clove Hitches   Neolithic Knots

3-4. Grouped fringes

Overcasting, cross-stitching, and *blanket stitching* (Fig. 3-2) focus on maintaining the woven edge without affecting—through grouping or any other alteration—the pure warp.

Simple *hemstitching* and *twining* (Fig. 3-3) barely group the warp ends. For these to be effective, the wrapping or twining should be done around the smallest number of warp threads. This applies particularly to twining, where the friction of thread twisted against thread is the only factor securing the woven edge.

Implicit in all these separate introductions of yarn is the option for an attention-getting edge definition achieved with the use of a different-colored or -textured material.

A more substantial division of warp fringe into separated groups can be achieved by *overhand knotting, vertical clove hitches,* or *neolithic knots* (Fig. 3-4). Overhand knotting is probably the most common edge-securing resolution. It is a simple, stable, relatively small knot tied directly by the warp ends and does not depend upon the addition of another element. It can be specifically placed by providing a barrier (pinching with thumb and forefinger) against which the tying loop can be tightened. Vertical clove hitches and their reverse side, neolithic knots, both involve use of independent tying cords.

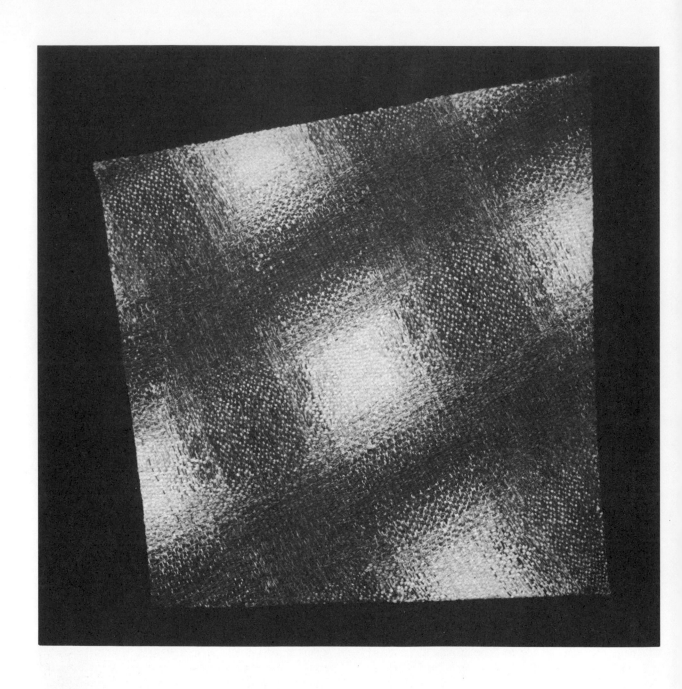

Herman Scholten
Ruit/1977
wool, linen, sisal
102" x 98" (260 x 250 cm.)

Plaids are normally stable and predictable geometric configurations. In Ruit (Check), the plaid is activated by virtue of the structural as well as the visual. A full range of weaves, from warp-face balanced to weft-face, intersect with and intercept each other to create the vibrating image.

The fabric is woven with thick yarns handled in groups to increase their physical scale. This augmentation in scale draws one to immediately focus on the thread groupings and follow their complex and irregular interactions. The bundled warp includes taut structural threads and loosely woven stragglers that wiggle across the surface, rendering it fluid and alive.

The angled rotation of the woven fabric, and the folding of its edges to eliminate the selvedges, creates an ambiguity between warp and weft. The odd, polygonal shape of the tapestry further challenges the even, steady concept of a plaid. (Photographs: Jeffrey Schiff, Boston)

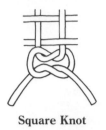

Square Knot

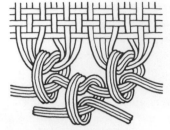

Repeated Half-Knots

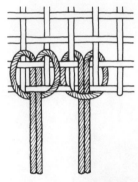

Lark's Head Addition

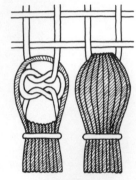

Tassels

3-5. Splayed and added fringes

Another treatment involves splaying the warp ends by tying them with single *square knots* or *repeated half-knots* (Fig. 3-5). If a fuller, more lush fringe is desirable, the existing fringe can be supplemented (or substituted) either by *lark's heads* (sometimes called *snitch knots*) of additional threads, or by the addition of *tassels.*

The *Philippine edge, locked loop,* (Fig. 3-6), and several other looped, braided, and woven edges (Fig. 3-7) can be used to shift the location of the warp threads before allowing them to fall. The Philippine edge creates a horizontal ridge on its front face; the locked loop and other loop-formed edges are visually more intricate and decorative.

All the methods discussed so far are worked directly against the edge of the weaving, leaving the emerging fringe in its original thread state. Another choice would be to organize and control the warp, giving it a tapelike or corded appearance. Cross-sectionally flat finishes (Fig. 3-8) include *kilim* (or woven slit) *tabs,* as well as various simple *sennits: 3-strand flat* (sometimes

SENNITS

Kilim Tabs

3-Strand Flat

4-Strand Flat

Square Knot

Decorative

3-8. Tapelike fringes

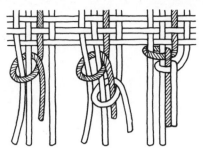

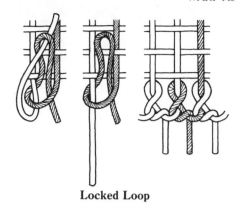

Philippine Edge

Locked Loop

3-6. Shifted fringes/1

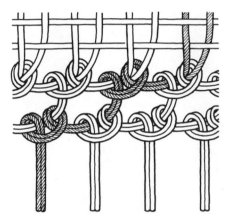

Looped Edges

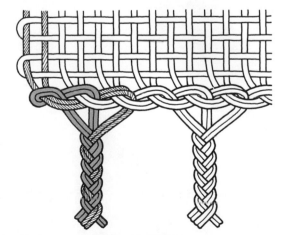

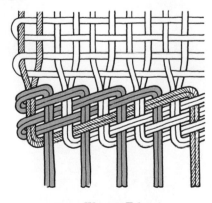

Woven Edge

Braided Edge

3-7. Shifted fringes/2

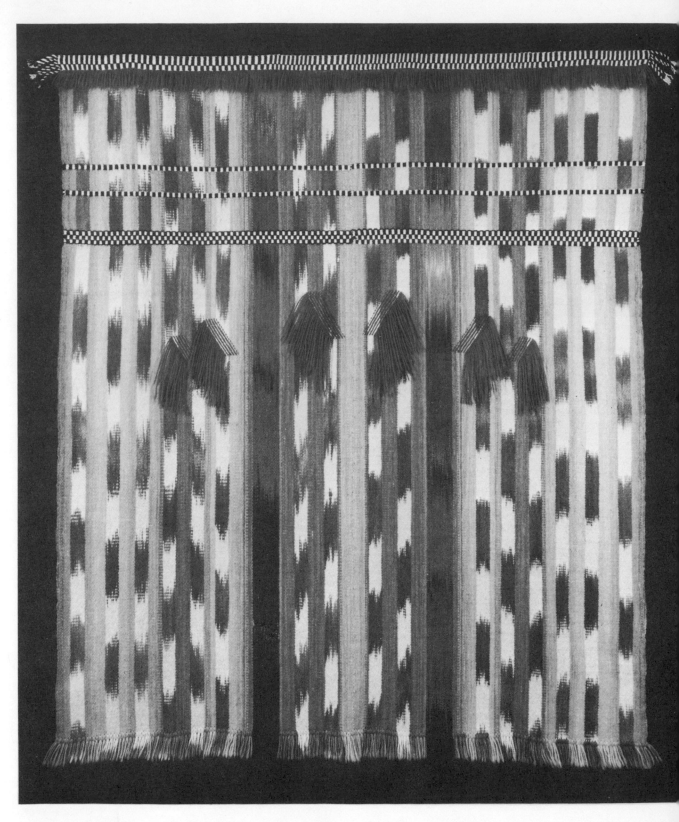

Alice Marcoux
Tyla's Blanket/*1982*
wool (ikat)
66" x 50" (167.5 x 127 cm.)

Tyla's Blanket *is a celebration of bright color and pattern. Its alternating arrangement of broad, ikatted warp-face stripes and equally wide, solid color warp-face bands has the joyful exuberance of a grossly enlarged Guate-* malan weaving. The irregular ikat pattern implies a grid, but never resolves into blocklike rigidity. Its fluid variability contrasts with the horizontal bands of precise, refined checkerboard, which suggest a playful African feeling. From this cross-cultural mix, three enigmatic pairs of paintbrushlike weft elements emerge. The weft yarns fall, freed from the confining mask of the warp-face weave, as if a diagonal incision were revealing the interior of the weaving. (Photographs: Cathy Carver, Providence, Rhode Island)

SENNITS

4-Strand Square

3-9. Corded fringes

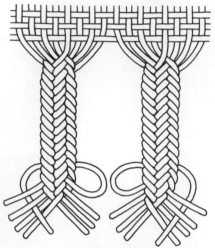

8-Strand Square

Alternate Crown

**Continuous
Right Crown**

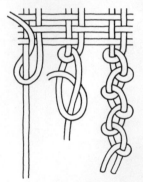

Alternate Hitches

3-10. Heavy corded fringe

3-11. Plying

called standard braid or plait), *4-strand flat, square knot,* and *decorative* braids. More cordlike, generally heavier, and potentially stiffer or more spiky finishes include: *4-* and *8-strand square sennits, alternate* or *continuous crown sennits* (Fig. 3-9), *alternate hitches* (Fig. 3-10), *plying* (Fig. 3-11), and *wrapping* (figure 3-14). Execution of most of these finishing methods is shown in the diagrams, and supplemented with the following information:

For *alternate hitches* (Fig. 3-10) to be an option, there must be considerable warp length available. When this technique is used, the finished cord is half as long as its original length. Alternate hitching creates a very thick cord—twice as heavy as one in which the same number of threads have been plied. This makes it useful for achieving a large scale with relatively few threads.

Plying the warp ends (Fig. 3-11) is accomplished by first separately overtwisting two groups of warp ends in the same direction and then letting them twist (or ply) together in the opposite way. For this method to hold, the direction of twist in the warp threads should be analyzed and that direction followed in the initial (overtwisting) step. The free end of the resulting

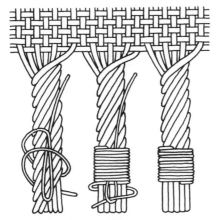
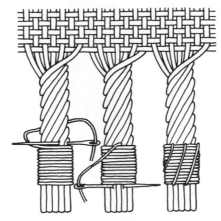

Common Whipping   **Palm-and-Needle Whipping**   **Snaked Whipping**

3-12. Cord-securing techniques/1

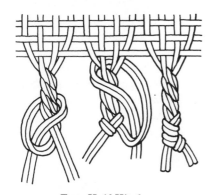

Two Half-Hitches   **Overhand Knot**

3-13. Cord-securing techniques/2

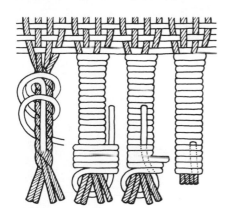

3-14. Wrapping

cord should be secured by *whipping* (Fig. 3-12), which will not change the cord's profile; tying two *half-hitches* (Fig. 3-13), which will slightly increase the cord's diameter; or *overhand knotting*, which will introduce a punctuating, beadlike element (Fig. 3-13).

Whipping (Fig. 3-12) and *wrapping* (Fig. 3-14) are terms for essentially the same technique. Whipping is a sailors' term for securing rope ends to keep them from unraveling. It generally connotes minimal coverage—from ¼ to 1 inch—whereas the term wrapping is used to describe the same activity worked over a larger area. The technique involves the consistent, slightly tensioned winding of a separate thread around a group of two or more warp ends. One thread is wound at a time, completely covering while slightly compressing the core of warp yarns. The color of the winding thread is seen purely and boldly. Shorter wrappings enable color changes that create stripes. Each wound thread should lie immediately next to— not on or away from—the preceding one. If done correctly, the wrapping rigidifies the ends, giving them body. Depending on the character of the core (and additions are always an option), the wrapped ends can be bent to take on a specific shape.

Warren Seelig
Vertical Shield #2/1976
cotton, Mylar strips
81" x 14" in. (205 x 36 cm.)

*Vertical Shield #2 is a formal, totemic, entirely mon-
ochromatic work whose image is created by the play of
light on shifting planes of woven cloth. It is made of
double-layer fabric casings tightly stretched like skins
around skeletal strips of sheet Mylar core. The fabric's
adhesion to its ribs causes the frontal plane of adjacent
casings to tilt slightly, permitting these planes to alternately catch and shed light, accentuating and contrasting
highlight and shadow. Emphasized by the light, the
hinged juncture between these planes takes on the appearance of a graphic outline.*

*By leaving every other pair of the central, horizontal
casings empty, the squarish shaped edge blocks are allowed to flute. A different crenulation is caused by sub-
dividing the middle casings—changing their shape into
blocks—and pinching together the outermost of these
blocks at both top and bottom edges of the piece. The use
of large-scale, textural cotton retains the sensual, tactile
quality of cloth despite the crisp, hard, paperlike character
of the folds. (Photographs courtesy Hadler/Rodriguez
Gallery, New York)*

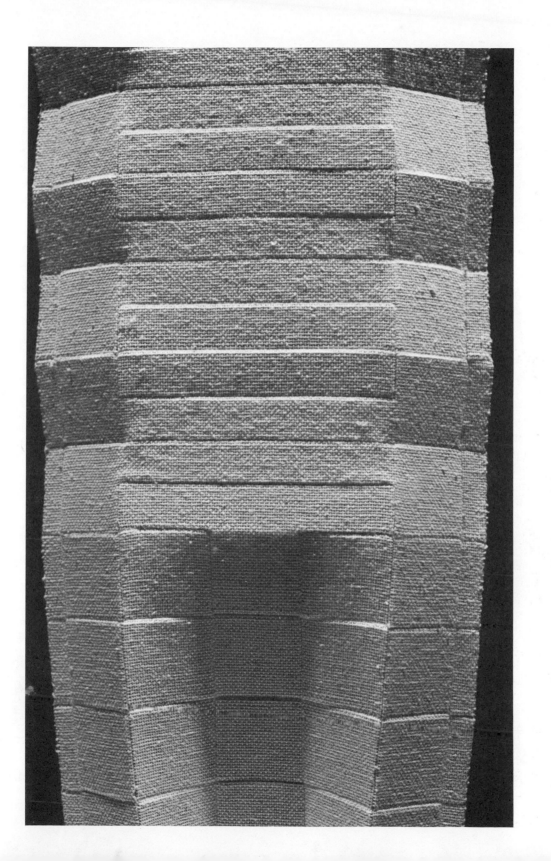

CLEAN FINISH EDGES

Fringeless finishes are almost exclusively worked with the integral warp ends. The edges formed by the various techniques range from thin and delicate to broad and substantial. All expose, to varying degrees, the pure warp color.

The Simple Edge

The simple edge, shown in Figure 3-15, is probably the easiest and quickest to make. It involves sewing alternate warp threads back into the weft (for approximately 1 inch), following the path of the adjacent warp yarn. Both sewn and loose ends can be cut at the points where they emerge from the woven cloth.

Although combining this sewing with close cropping works well with pure weft-face and allows the piece to be reversible, it is not universally applicable. The sewn warp will be clearly visible in all other weave types; the act of sewing will become too difficult in pure warp-face; and with the warp densities in between, the revealed sewn lengths will become prominent visual elements. Whatever the weave type, sewing in the warp ends essentially doubles the warp's original bulk. This must be planned for in advance (by overgenerous weft arching) because without adequate provision, the weaving will buckle and draw in at both selvedges.

Band Edges

Where reversibility is desirable, but warp sewing is not, the *woven* and *braided edges* shown in Figure 3-16 might be tried. In both of these, the edge formed

is a relatively broad addition to the weaving. The ends are radically displaced before they escape, and are cut off at the edge farthest away from the weaving. To keep the band rectangular, an additional yarn or yarns must be worked in at the beginning.

Although a second type of *woven edge* (Fig. 3-17) and its more textural variations—*soumak* and *twined edge* (Fig. 3-18)—are clearly related to the first woven and braided edges, their ends wind up facing upward rather than down and their emerging warp ends overlap the loom-woven portion of the work. These ends can be eliminated by sewing them in or pushing them through to the back, tacking them under a couple of

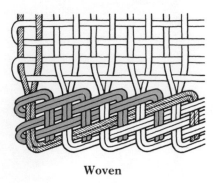

Woven

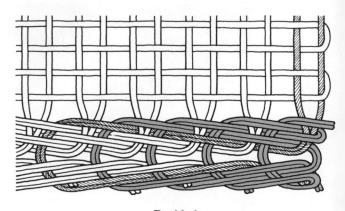

Braided

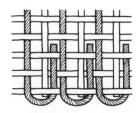

3-15. Simple (fringeless) edge

3-16. Woven/braided edges (unsewn ends)

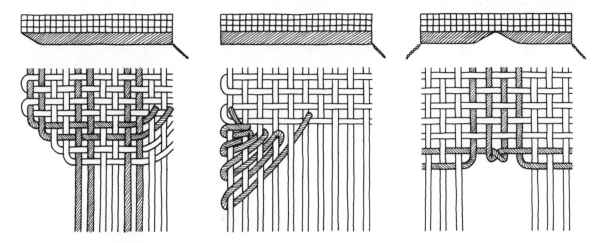

3-17. Band-forming edges: woven (ends sewn in)

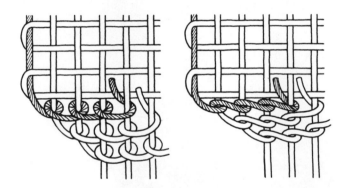

Soumak Edge

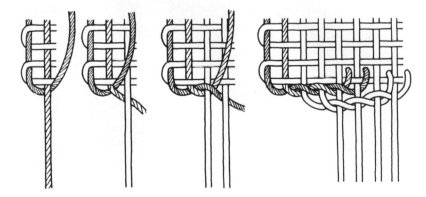

Twined Edge

3-18. Band-forming edges: nonwoven (ends sewn in)

Michelle Héon
Robe de Cérémonie 1/*1982*
linen, rayon, silk, cotton paper
78" x 48" (198 x 122 cm.)

Robe de Cérémonie 1 *is at once both beautiful and disturbing. Its human-sized kimono shape refers to the refined civilization and traditional order of Japanese culture, while its fragmented edges and dissolving, tattered cloth, reinforced by a layer of cast paper, bring to mind the disintegration of a society. The fabric's uniformly weakened condition suggests an insidious cause for its deterioration. The kimono's front edge appears decoratively scalloped while having the characteristic shrivel and darkened color of charred and melted nylon cloth. The work seems to be either a specter of apocalypse, or a record of past devastation.*

The surface of the work is enriched by being woven in various weaves. All of the cloth's edges wave from relaxed warp tension and are reinforced by pure weft-face weaving. The darker weft is used both to define edges and to give the effect of shadows elsewhere in the cloth. The central section of each part of the garment's lengths is woven in balanced weave, in keeping with the traditional weave type for clothing. Variations in the warp/weft balance alter the color throughout the fabric. (Photographs: Gilles Morisette, Quebec)

wefts, and then cutting them, leaving short tails. If these ends are not tacked or if long tails are left, the ends will succumb to gravity and form fringe.

In all five edges, the warp ends function as warps and wefts. Usually, each individual warp acts as a weft for only a short distance, but if each warp thread continues to function as a weft across the full width of the cloth, the profile of the fabric's bottom (or top) edge will slant diagonally. (*Note:* To do this, you must have extremely long warp ends to work with.) The effect of this will be dramatic. You should realize, however, that the finish will be time consuming and will only postpone final resolution of the warp fringe. Basically, this activity will redirect the warp ends so that they emerge from the cloth horizontally.

If, instead, you wish to create a uniform band, then the number of times each warp yarn is interlaced should be limited. The full band width is reached when the final warp yarn that acts like a weft is the same yarn as the last one to receive an interweaving weft.

These finishes can be started on either side or from knotted warp ends somewhere (generally exactly) in the center of the weaving. They begin angled, with a wedge shape missing because of the warp-becomes-weft role switching. This void can be filled by the initial use of an independent weft yarn. After completing any of these edge bands and reaching the opposite side (or sides), one is left with several unworkable ends. These can be finished with any of the controlled fringe techniques (Figs. 3-8 through 3-14).

Narrow Finishes

The remaining methods are all narrow finishes that are either circular (Figs. 3-19 and 3-20) or flat (Figs. 3-21 and 3-22) in appearance. All are started on one side and continued across the width of the fabric. The most consistent results will be obtained by completing each edge in one sitting.

The *Maori edge* (Fig. 3-19) gives a tight rolled finish that looks best on its reverse side. It should therefore be worked on the back of the cloth. The starting sequence (see diagram) involves only the first four warp ends and is not repeated. Repetition of the remaining three steps creates the edge.

The *4-strand sennit edge* (Fig. 3-20) has a similar but somewhat bulkier appearance, owing to the addition of a separate yarn. This yarn should be relatively heavy and at least twice the length of the edge to be finished.

The *Taniko edge* (Fig. 3-21) has angled ridges but is broader and flatter than both the Maori and 4-strand sennit edges. It is worked with two additional yarns that have been first folded in half and then locked with each other. Each of these yarns is approximately three times the desired finished length of the edge.

Double knot, chained loops, and *edge braiding* (Fig. 3-22) are all self-tying, fairly quick finishing methods.

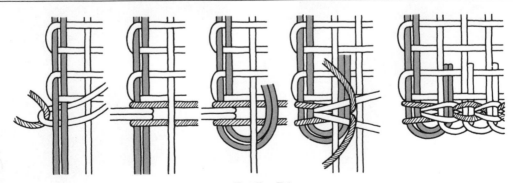

3-21. Flat edge finish/1

Taniko Edge

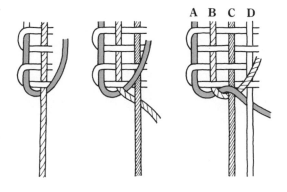

A B C D

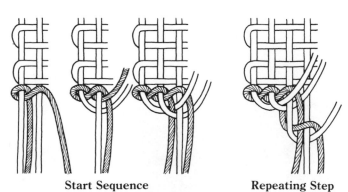

Step 1   Step 2   Step 3

A

(New B)

(New A)

D   B   C

(New C) (New D)

Start Sequence

Maori Edge

Continuing Sequence
(In Step 3, threads are relettered
in preparation for the repeat of Step 1)

3-19. Narrow rolled finish/1

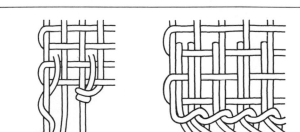

Start Sequence   **Repeating Step**

4-Strand Sennit Edge

3-20. Narrow rolled finish/2

Double Knot

Chained Loops

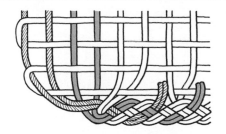

Edge Braiding

3-22. Flat edge finishes/2

Mollie Fletcher
Apron/*1981*
linen
18″ x 23″ (46 x 58 cm.)

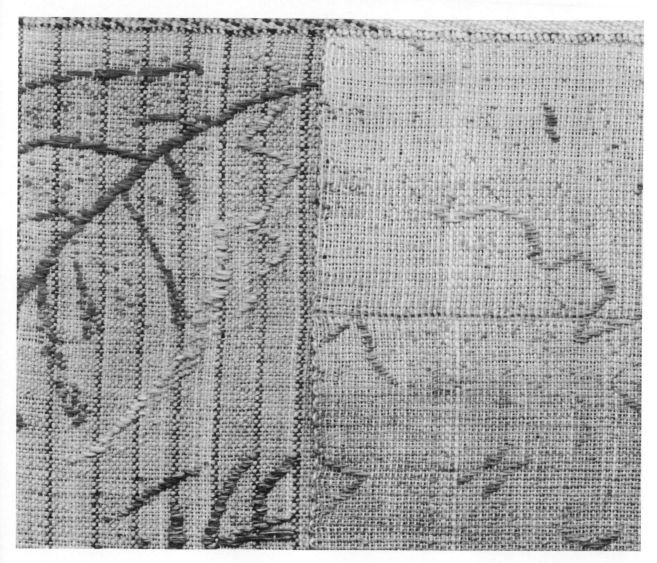

In Apron, *a double-layer central section sits in front of a much broader background layer, occasionally pinching back to join this underlayer in shared-weft seams. The color of the central section gradually deepens in correspondence with the compressed intervals of these seams, the combined effect suggesting the loss of natural light and increase in pressure under water. The sense of penetrability yet supportiveness associated with water is enhanced by supplementary floating imagery. These figurative elements consist of variably sized fluid lines that refer to primal life forms. Their location in the tapestry is erratic. The lines seem to move both across and on* the surface, while their fragmentation implies their immersion within it. The awareness of the underlying layer increases the spatial ambiguity.

The ground cloth extends to the sides and there the contrast between the organic and geometric is crystallized. The supplementary weft marks assume more developed branchlike forms, although their color remains nonliteral. These branches are equally rootless and float, but against a more specifically patterned field. The rich, visually active surface of Apron *is the result of the natural tension between these disparate elements. (Photographs: Shel Hensleigh, Detroit)*

Two HANDLING THE WARP

4 The Loom

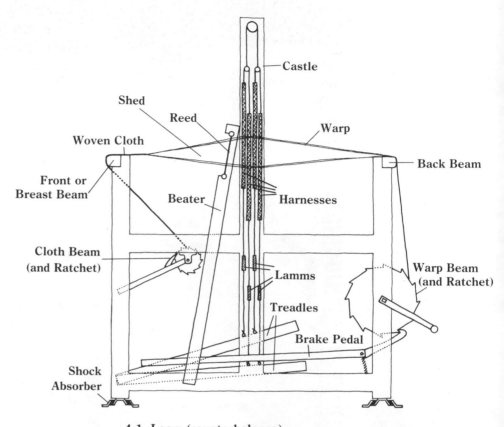

4-1. Loom (counterbalance)

A loom (Fig. 4-1) is a simple machine for handling warp. It provides organized storage for the warp, establishes and maintains warp tension, facilitates warp manipulation, assists in regularized packing of the weft—which standardizes the woven grid—and provides storage for the finished cloth.

The warp begins its association with the loom by having its extra length wound onto the *warp beam*. From there it passes over the *back beam* and heads for the *castle*.

Within the castle are *harnesses*—separate, parallel frames that can change in their vertical relationship to one another. Harnesses are the essential components of a loom; the mechanism for their change distinguishes the different loom types. On the most general level, if harness change is foot-instigated—by stepping on treadles (or pedals)—the loom is a *floor loom;* if change is brought about by hand manipulation of levers, then the loom is a *table loom*. More specifically, if the primary action of the harness shafts is downward, or sinking, thereby causing other shafts to rise, the change is based on a straightforward pulley mechanism, and the loom is considered *counterbalanced*. If initial harness action is upward, or rising, the lift is caused by the mechanically generated upward push (or pull) of the jack mechanism in a *jack loom*. And finally, if the harnesses move in both directions simultaneously,

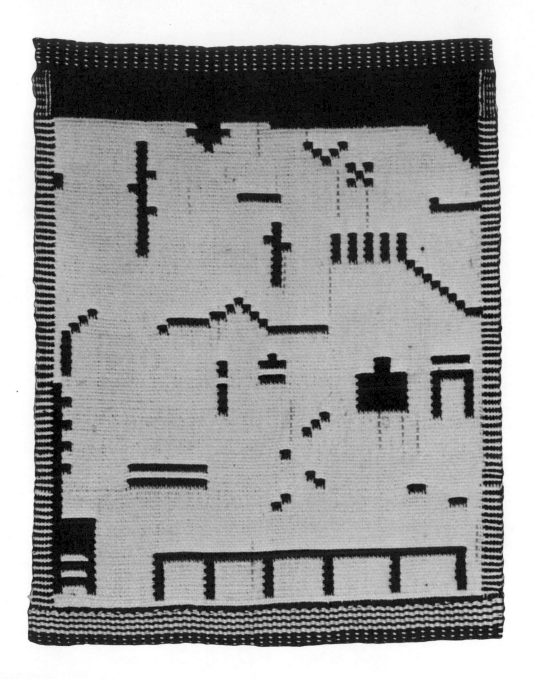

Sandra Brownlee-Ramsdale
Woodward Series #2/1980
cotton, nylon
10" x 8" (25 x 20 cm.)

The intimate scale of Woodward Series #2 *intentionally suggests a journal page. According to Brownlee-Ramsdale, the weaving "refers to a kind of mark-making that is both personal (a written signature) and mechanical (the natural outgrowth of loom generated imagery, integral to woven cloth)." The work's small size fits comfortably between the loom's breast beam and beater, enabling uninterrupted vision of the piece throughout the weaving process.*

The technique used is a double-weave pick-up which allows the bold graphic imagery to develop simply, quickly, and linearly. The loom is seen as analogous to a simple computer with its imaging capability locked within the scale and rectangular format of the warp/weft elements or pixel grid. The warp is randomly marked by painting a stripe on the yarn while it is still on the cone. These brief visual zips have the quality of electrical interference and animate the woven field. (Photographs: Jack Ramsdale, Toronto)

a more complicated pulley and double lamm system is in effect in a *countermarche loom.*

Within the harnesses and attached to them are *heddles,* independent vertical members made of either metal or string, that have centrally placed, relatively small openings called *eyes.* The warp yarns are attached to different harnesses by being individually threaded through separate heddle eyes (Fig. 4-2).

After being threaded, the warp yarns continue their parallel paths to the *beater* and are sleyed in the reed. The *reed* is a slotted metal grate set vertically within the beater. The threads are drawn through its regular spaces, or *dents,* which maintain the threads in a set order and density.

Beyond the reed, the warp threads are tightly tied to the *apron rod* extension of the *cloth beam.* Once the warp threads have been uniformly tensioned and secured, the weaving can begin.

Weaving is the right-angle intersection of two linear elements passing sequentially over and under each other. The process is made physically simpler by using harnesses. Changing the vertical relationship of the harnesses creates two separate warp planes: one above, the other below. The wedge-shaped, tentlike space formed between them is called the *shed,* and it is into this that the weft is inserted. Creation of the shed expedites the weaving process by allowing the weft to make a smooth and direct transit through the warp. Without a shed, the weft would have to tediously find its way.

The sequence in which the warp threads connect with the harnesses is called the *threading pattern.* The order in which the harnesses are raised and lowered is the *treadling pattern.* All the threads attached to a harness are called into action whenever that harness is activated. Because threads cannot change harnesses, the threading pattern determines the loom-assisted potential for warp/weft relationships. The treadling pattern, by enabling the insertion of the weft, finalizes the weave construction.

The weft is neatly and uniformly packed into position when the shed is closed and the *reed/beater* pulled through the warp. The reed packs the weft perpendicularly to the warp and thus keeps the weaving square.

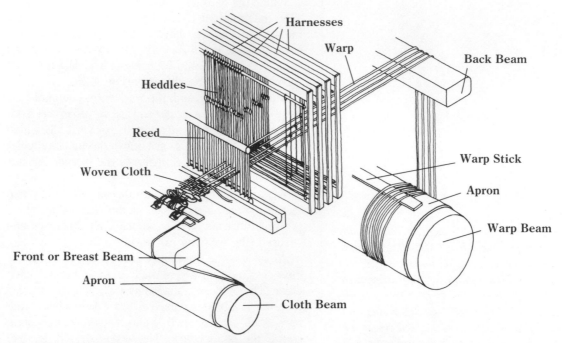

4-2. Parts of the loom directly involved with the warp

The resulting woven cloth passes over the *breast beam,* is wound on to the *cloth beam,* and is stored there until the weaving is completed.

LOOM LOSS FACTOR
The full warp length can never be completely woven. Approximately 1 yard—or slightly less for small table looms and more for deeper-castled, eight or more harness looms—is lost to the loom. Part of this yard is used in the beginning to tie knots; the rest becomes unusable at the warp's end when the remaining length no longer allows the harnesses to separate and form a shed. These unweavable lengths are not waste: When the weaving has been removed from the loom, they are used in the selected finishing method.

LOOM MODIFICATIONS
While looms are basically straightforward and their parts and action can be simply explained, their physical

engineering should not be underestimated. The loom's outer structure must be sufficiently rigid to resist the compressive force of the warp under tension, yet also include movable parts (warp and cloth beams). Its inner structure (harnesses, lamms, treadles) must be capable of significant vertical movement in spite of the warp's tensioned resistance. In other words, management of the warp is not as simple as it appears. Loom performance can be improved—or at least the odds weighted in its favor—by making a few initial adjustments.

In most looms, both cloth and apron rods are generally made from relatively thin, circular stock. When warps that are narrower than the length of these rods are wound on them, these rods frequently bend. This bending, if extreme, can create tensioning problems. The bent rods also offer variable edges rather than consistent ones, causing the warp threads to assume different lengths. The differences are further compounded when the bent rods do not roll evenly around the beams. Replacing these rods with broad, flat, non-bending bars corrects the problem.

Looms with cloth aprons are often initially outfitted with two rods per apron, while looms with string aprons have just one rod each. The attachment of an additional rod to the warp beam apron rod(s) greatly eases the later attachment of the warp when beaming "back to front."

Harness change during weaving is often noisy and physically jolting. Attaching industrial shock absorbers to the loom's feet siphons off the repetitive shock and vibration, thereby reducing strain on loom joints, bolts, weaver, and downstairs neighbors.

And, finally, weighting the beater by attaching a heavy steel bar that spans the beater's length enhances the weaver's ability to weave. A heavy beater enables the weft to be firmly packed by gentle beating action, rather than by the usual abrasive slamming. Slamming causes "loom walking," in which the sheer force of each successive beat steadily propels both loom and weaver backwards across the floor. The gentle beating

made possible by a weighted beater is better for the loom, the weaver, and the warp.

WEAVING TOOLS

There are a few additional, far smaller, hand-held weaving tools that should be mentioned at this point (Fig. 4-3). These assist with either handling the warp in preparation for or managing the weft during weaving.

The *heddle hook* facilitates the drawing of warp threads through the heddle eyes; either its unnotched back side or an *S-* or *reed hook* can be used to do the same thing (sleying) through the dents in the reed.

Shuttles are vessels for organizing, storing, and ultimately transporting weft yarns through the open shed.

The *temple,* an adjustable-length, hinged device with spiky claws at its extremities, can be used to maintain selvedge width. Its use is discussed in chapter 6, Arch Problems.

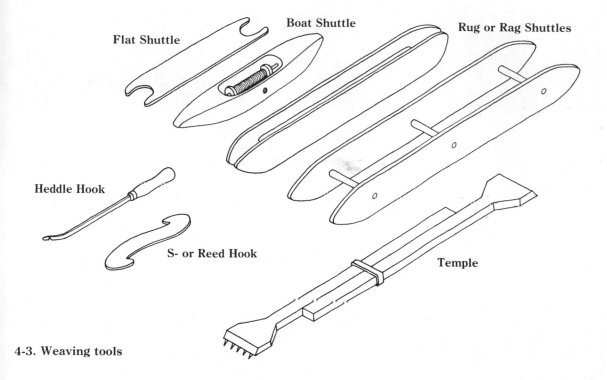

Flat Shuttle   **Boat Shuttle**   **Rug or Rag Shuttles**

Heddle Hook

S- or Reed Hook

Temple

4-3. Weaving tools

Cynthia Schira
warp experiment/1983
Perle cotton, cotton floss, rayon
Area shown: 12" x 15" (30 x 38 cm.)

This experimental fragment is woven by using a computerized loom to facilitate drawing upon a multitude of complex weave structures. Rich variety is built into the surface. Three independent layers of warp are called on, alternately functioning as the structural warp and supplementary warp elements. Their trade off enables the fluid creation of amorphous shapes both on top of and within the weaving. More linear and less dense supplementary wefts partially obscure the densely woven ground, adding yet another compositional and dimensional layer to the charged field. The inherent flexibility of these many layers allows spontaneous forms to be simply integrated into the structure of the cloth. (Photograph: Pok-Chi-Lau, Lawrence, Kansas)

5 Warping: Dressing the Loom

Once basic warp decisions have been made, there are two fundamentally different methods by which cones of yarn can be transformed into a warp and transferred to the loom.

The first method is so much more commonly used by handweavers that it is referred to simply as *warp winding* or, generically, as *warping*. It is a two-step system involving initial hand winding of the warp and subsequent beaming onto the loom. It is economical in amount and cost of equipment, which is limited to warping board or reel, lease sticks, and possibly raddle; requires less set-up time, making it faster to use for warps between 2 and 20 yards, although it can be used for longer ones; and is suitable for either complex (varied yarns) or simple (one yarn) warps.

The second method, *sectional warping*, combines the two steps by enabling the warp to be wound directly onto the beam. Sectional warping involves more work in setting up and requires considerably more equipment: sectional warp beam, tension box, yarn counter (optional), various dent reeds, spool rack, bobbins or spools, and bobbin or spool winder. Yet in spite of this, it can be more practical and efficient for warps that are extremely long (20 or more yards) and is the method often used by production weavers.

Warping, however executed, is the necessary preliminary step before the loom can be dressed. *Dressing the loom* is the inclusive, general term covering the two essential processes of *beaming* (winding of the excess warp length onto the warp beam) and *threading* (affixing the warp yarns to different harnesses and establishing their density by drawing them through the reed). These two steps can be undertaken in either order. When beaming at the back of the loom precedes threading from the front, the process is called *dressing from "back to front."* If, instead, the warp is threaded first and its length beamed afterwards, then it is called *dressing from "front to back."*

In this chapter, for the sake of clarity and useful continuity, these steps are presented in the following order: (1) Basic warping, which is the prerequisite for either complete method of loom dressing, is explained first, then (2) both loom dressing methods are briefly compared. (3) All phases of loom dressing "back to front," including techniques for one-person and two-person beaming, are described next, followed by (4) a discrete presentation of dressing the loom "front to back." (5) Sectional warping, which combines warp winding with the beaming half of loom dressing, is outlined last. Because sectional warping/beaming is essentially a variation on the "back to front" method, you should follow the procedure described in the earlier "back to front" section for instructions on threading.

BASIC WARPING

WARPING BOARD/WARPING REEL
For yarns to become a functional warp, they must be organized into a set of parallel threads of uniform length. Either a warping board or warping reel provides a simple and relatively compact means for carrying out this task.

A *warping board* is a rectangular frame with pegs protruding from it. The pegs on its two vertical sides are placed at regular intervals large enough to allow a fisted hand to fit between them; two additional pegs are placed close together toward the center of either (or both) horizontal side. Ideally, and generally, a warping board measures 1 yard across. As warping boards are simple to make, a useful addition to most would be the central placement of another vertical

member with holes for pegs drilled at the same regular intervals as the pegs on the frame's vertical sides. Inserting a peg in one of these holes facilitates the winding of a final half yard.

Warping reels are essentially four-sided revolving warping boards. They have two horizontal cross bars with pegs placed in roughly the same positions as on the warping board. The placement of these bars is adjustable, both vertically and horizontally, so they can be moved up and down and placed on different sides. Warping reels come in various sizes: table models measure 2 yards around; floor models measure upwards of 3 or 4 yards.

The use of either is a matter of personal preference. Warping reels require less physical effort in winding a warp and for that reason are particularly helpful in winding long warps. The larger floor reels can be as efficient as the sectional beaming method for winding extremely long warps. On the other hand, all warping reels take up more space than warping boards do, and the smaller table models need to have their bases firmly secured to a horizontal surface to prevent them from constantly falling over.

Because winding warps can be physically straining, the exact location for either the warping board or reel should be considered carefully and individually. You should determine the correct height for the top horizontal cross-piece of either by raising your arm and finding the maximum height at which it can be comfortably maintained. This generally hovers a few inches below shoulder height. If frequent long warps necessitate excessive bending to reach lower pegs, the board or reel should be raised slightly, approaching, but never exceeding, shoulder height.

WINDING A WARP
(*Note:* The following directions are written, and the diagrams drawn, assuming right-handedness. Left-handed weavers should substitute left for right, counterclockwise for clockwise in the text, and read the diagrams reversed in a mirror.)

Begin by making a good-sized loop with the free end of the warp yarn and securing it with an overhand

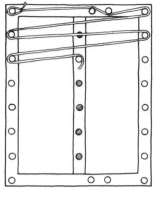
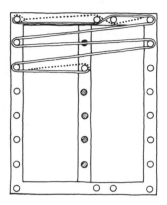

Warping Board

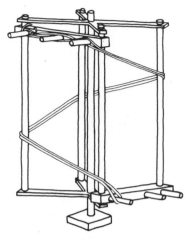

Warping Reel

5-1. The path of the first two threads

knot. This loop is placed around the peg in the upper left-hand corner of the warping board, or the farthest left peg on the top cross bar of the warping reel (Fig. 5-1). These pegs are the starting point for winding the warp. The yarn follows the path indicated in the diagram, moving toward the horizontally paired pegs. The yarn passes over the first peg and under the second, and continues winding around the warping reel when it is spun clockwise, or zigzags back and forth around each peg on alternate sides of the warping board, until the desired length has been reached. At this point, one thread has been wound. *(Note:* This route can be staked out by a *guide thread* before winding the first warp yarn. The guide thread is premeasured to the desired warp length, but it is not part of, and should not resemble, the warp. If you are using a warping reel, a guide thread is necessary to establish the angle of the warp's course. Otherwise, variations in the angle will significantly alter the yarn's length.)

To wind the next warp yarn, the direction of winding is reversed by looping around the last (or ending) peg reached by the first thread and retracing the steps up to the paired pegs. Again, the yarn passes over the first peg it encounters and under the next. The yarn then continues on the lower course until it reaches the starting peg. At this point, two threads have been wound, and a single crossing in their paths (between the paired pegs) becomes evident.

This crossing is known as the *lease,* the *cross,* or, as it is graphically called, the *X.* This *X* is the only means by which the order of the threads can be maintained. This order is crucial: All the subsequent steps in setting up the loom depend upon it, so make sure that each pair of warp yarns re-creates this *X.*

The winding continues, alternately following the path of these first two threads. Wind the yarn by pulling horizontally with a very slight tension. Be careful not to tug the yarn—the tension exerted is cumulative and, in time, will cause either warping board pegs or warping reel uprights to bend. The bent pegs or uprights will effectively reduce the length of the yarn's course, causing the yarns to wind on in progressively shorter lengths, and one of the main purposes for using the warping board or reel—the measuring of yarns to the same length—will be undermined.

When winding warp on a warping board, use both arms to expedite the winding and reduce the fatigue otherwise experienced by the winding arm and shoulder blade. Instead of swaying gently and twisting slightly as the yarn is placed over the pegs, keep your body relatively straight and centered in front of the warping board and directly over the yarn. Pull the yarn vertically (not diagonally) with your right hand, loosely catch it with your left, and, with both hands, simultaneously pull it toward both sides of the warping board. Use both hands to gently hook the yarn over

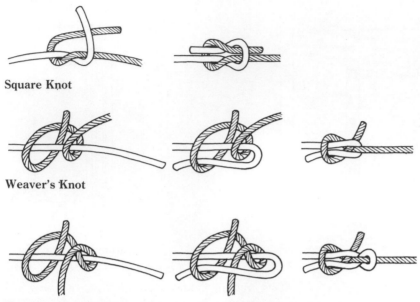

Square Knot

Weaver's Knot

Double Weaver's Knot

5-2. Square and weaver's knots

the next pegs on both sides. Next, carry the yarn back toward the center with your right hand and then repeat the expansion with both hands simultaneously. When you reach the crossing pegs, create the X with your right hand. Then transfer the yarn to your left hand, carry it out to the starting peg and back to center, and pass it back to your right hand. These basic steps are alternated throughout winding.

The winding of the warp should be interrupted if a flaw in the yarn—a knot, weak spot, or textural abberation—is discovered. These yarn flaws are often responsible for broken threads or poor tension areas later on. Unwind the yarn from the flaw to either the starting or ending peg, whichever is closer. Eliminate the flaw by first cutting the yarn so it extends 2 to 3 inches beyond the peg, and then cutting again just beyond the flaw. Then tie the free, now flawless end to the cut warp end with either a square or weaver's knot (Fig. 5-2). This knot will never enter into the weavable portion of the warp because of its placement at the very beginning or end of the warp's length. This method of cutting and tying can be used to add more yarn or to change the warp to create warp stripes.

The winding of the warp stops when either the intended number of warp yarns have been wound or the pegs of either the warping board or reel become too full to accept additional yarns. At this point, tie another good-sized nonslip loop that will reach around the starting peg into the yarn. Place this loop around the peg, and cut the tail of the knot.

SECURING THE WARP

Ties of strong yarn immediately distinguishable from the warp threads are secured around the warp in the following places (Fig. 5-3):

1. *The X.* Since the X is the single most important aspect in warp preparation, it should be tied first. The tie encircles the X, traveling in the wedge-shaped spaces between the crossing line of the threads and the X-pegs to each side. The tie follows a U-shaped path down the length of one peg, crosses behind all the warp threads (just in front of the guide thread), and returns following the opposite peg. Knot both ends of the tie together with a square knot, square knot bow, or overhand

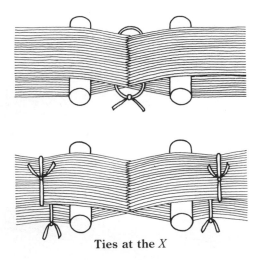

Ties at the *X*

Warp Beginning   *X*

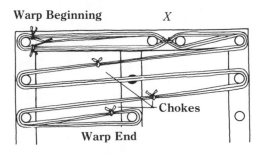

Chokes

Warp End

5-3. Securing the warp

knot. Instead of using the single-tie method just described, you can make four separate ties, one around each of the four warp groups created by the crossing pegs. If you are particularly nervous about fumbling this step, then five ties, following both methods, can be tied. It is far preferable to oversecure the *X* than to risk losing it.

2. *Warp beginning.* This tie travels down the length of, and actually touches, the starting peg. Its path should be clear and unobstructed and lie within the large tied loops. Both ends of the tie should be pulled together above the warp plane and tied tightly with a large bow. An additional tie (optional) can be inserted following the same course and tied below. The second tie pulls down the tied warp loops, visually clearing the path of the peg.

3. *Warp end.* The end of the warp is tied off with a single tie in the same manner as the warp's beginning. There is no need for a second tie.
4. *Chokes.* These are tightly tied bows that are temporarily secured around the whole warp at either 1- or 2-yard intervals. They grip the warp and prevent the threads from shifting.

WARP-WINDING TRICKS

Winding warps is never enjoyable (although composing them can be) and, physical strain aside, having to continually count is perhaps the most tedious part. Fortunately, with a simple warp, you need not count every thread. Winding can just proceed and occasionally be interrupted to make a count. As every round trip of warp yarns marks two threads, only half of the total (providing the last thread wound completes the circuit) need be actually counted and that sum doubled. The warp is clearly divided in halves at two places: surrounding the *X* and encompassing the ending peg. The counted yarns can be temporarily tied (with chokes) and the quantity noted.

If the expected loom-dressing method will be "back to front," the beaming phase of that method can be expedited by tying off 3- to 4-inch sections of warp threads at both their warp ends and around their middles with chokes.

To save time, you can wind two threads simultaneously if you carry both with the same hand (without switching back and forth between hands) and always keep them separate by holding a finger between them. This separation is necessary to keep the threads from plying with each other. If the two threads are different in color or texture, they can share the same lease—their differences will distinguish them later for threading purposes. If the two threads are the same, then some special finger and wrist work (which is best figured out individually) must be used to alternate the threads when forming the *X*. This will create a second *X* (between the crossing pegs and starting peg), which should be ignored.

Warping paddles exist to further increase the speed in which warps can be wound. Personally, I neither use nor recommend them. Losing hand contact when

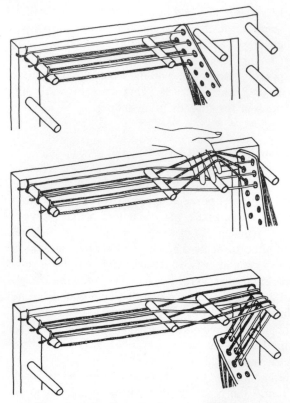

Forming the X on the Downward Path

Forming the X on the Return (Upward) Path

5-4. Using a warping paddle

winding the warp makes it much easier to let yarn flaws pass unnoticed. Additionally, tangles at the warp ends are inherent in this method. Each consecutive yarn at the X must cross paths with the total number of threads being carried by the paddle when the yarns are passed around the starting peg before returning to the X. This means that later, if "back to front" beaming is used, these threads can be only roughly straightened around the warp rod. (If the tangle is severe, the ends will have to be cut and retied after raddling. To compensate for these knots, an additional 6 inches should be figured into the warp length.) In a warp with a repeating sequence of three or more different yarns, however, using a warping paddle may be the only reasonable way—other than using a sectional warping method—to wind the warp. The tech-

nique is shown in the diagrams (Fig. 5-4).

Whichever technique you choose will be made easier by placing coned or spooled yarns on cone stands, or balled yarn in buckets. Use of stands or buckets prevents the yarn from rolling away, tangling with other yarns, and getting soiled.

REMOVING THE WARP: CHAINING
Warps are traditionally *chained* as they are removed from the board or reel to condense their length for ease in handling. Warp chaining is the same as chaining in crochet, but here you use a hand instead of a crochet hook. Chaining begins at the end of the warp farthest from the X. (Fig. 5-5).

To chain the warp, gently pull the tied warp end off the peg, and insert your right hand through the loop,

Starting Step	Repeating Sequence

5-5. Warp chaining

momentarily wearing the warp like a bracelet. Next, grab the warp a short distance ahead with your right hand, and, with your left hand, pull the loop off your wrist and down over your right hand. Then, pulling back the right thumb, join it with the rest of the hand and tuck the whole hand under the warp; push through. Once this is done, the right hand will again be wearing a warp loop bracelet. This procedure is repeated until just before the X is reached.

At that point, the chaining simply stops, and the empty hand is pulled out. The end of the warp is intentionally not pulled through. When correctly done, the chaining should dissolve when the warp is pulled from the X-end. If pulling creates a knot, then the X-end of the warp has been mistakenly pulled through, and it should be quickly pulled back out.

Once the chained warp has been removed from the board or reel, it is taken to either the front or back side of the loom, depending on which loom dressing method is chosen.

LOOM DRESSING: "BACK TO FRONT" VS. "FRONT TO BACK"

Dressing the loom *"back to front"* is a method suitable for all yarns—textured or smooth, strong or weak. Any width warp can be beamed alone (allowing the weaver to be self-sufficient), or narrow warps may be beamed more quickly with the help of a second person. The extra equipment required is both minimal and simple to make; limited to a *raddle* (a long, smooth, rectangular board, similar in width to the back beam, but generally flatter, that has simple dividers, or nails, placed at 1-inch intervals); a pair of *lease sticks* (equally

sized wooden slats with holes drilled at each end); and either *warp sticks* (long wooden slats similar to lease sticks but without drilled holes) or heavy paper.

Dressing the loom *"front to back"*, which must be done by two people, requires either one or two pairs of lease sticks or lease cords; optional *lary sticks* (identical long flat bars that span the length from front to back beam); and either warp sticks or heavy paper. It is a method suitable for strong, smooth yarns and is perhaps more workable than "back to front" for achieving a uniform tension with sticky yarns, such as some spun silks, or evenly textured but fibrous "hairy" wools. "Front to back" should not be used with any yarn that is fragile, extremely textural, or lacking in resilience. With textural yarns, the yarn shape variations in irregularly spun (slub), overspun (crepe), woven (chenille), wrapped (gimp), or novelty (loop and seed) yarns can easily catch in the heddles and stretch, weaken, and break. With a low-resilience yarn, such as linen, any thread that is caught momentarily will stretch, not return to its original length, and thus beam inconsistently.

"BACK TO FRONT"

Beaming
ATTACHING THE WARP
Begin by placing the X end of the warp at the back of the loom and throwing the bulk of the warp toward the front over the harnesses or castle.

The X is recorded by the sequential insertion of the two lease sticks, each one following a side of the tie at the X exactly. The lease sticks are suspended from the castle to hang evenly at heddle-eye height. To simplify this hanging and save time, make and use permanent lease suspension cords—two same-size cord loops that can be lark's-headed onto the top of the castle. The top lease stick rests in these loops after following the X-cord on the upper side of the X. The second lease stick traces the X-cord's lower path, and then the two sticks are tied together. The ties each follow a figure-8 path (the same end is put through each lease stick hole in the same direction). This figure-8 automatically spaces the lease sticks and keeps them parallel. Tie the strings with square knots, allowing for a ½-inch separation between the two sticks.

Position a raddle, that is longer than the width of the proposed warp centrally on top of the back beam, and tie it in place. Bring the shorter end of the warp across the raddle in a roughly straight manner and slip it onto the warp rod. Make sure that the warp groups are attached in order and that the yarns within them are not twisted. Tie the warp and apron rods together at their ends, and then temporarily suspend them from the back beam.

At this point, the ties at the X should be rechecked to verify that the X has been faithfully recorded by the lease sticks. The warp loops and individually tied threads of each warp group should be reexamined to make sure that each is secured around the warp rod. After any nonconforming threads are corrected, the warp ties can be removed.

DISTRIBUTING THREADS IN THE RADDLE
At this point, the threads must be distributed in the correct order and quantity across the raddle. Count the threads out in the same sequence as they were originally wound on the warping board—in other words, the order maintained by the lease sticks. To determine which thread follows which other, gently separate the warp threads sideways. The thread that moves freely, without interference to its sideways movement, is the next thread in the sequence. Successive threads should be coming from alternate positions—over/under and under/over—in the lease sticks. Since the warp is generally centered on the loom, the raddle should be checked to see that it is centered on the back beam. Starting from the raddle's center divider, count half the total number of inches

of actual warp width in the raddle spaces. The space arrived at in the count is the beginning slot for the warp's distribution; the first inch, or partial inch, of threads will be placed there.

When a warp does not have a selvedge treatment involving density change, the threads can be distributed evenly in the raddle according to the standard density. For example, a warp that is 14 inches wide with a density of 16 threads to the inch would be spread in the raddle as follows. Since half of 14 is 7, count out to the seventh slot and place the first 16 threads in that space. Position the next 16 threads in the next slot, and so on, until all the threads are placed.

When there is a special selvedge treatment, yarn distribution in the first and final slots is affected. Another example: The weaving width is a full 12 inches with 20 threads to the inch and there are two ¼-inch double density selvedges. In this case, the first and final slots are both sixth from the center and each have ¾ inch worth of threads at a density of 20 threads per inch (=15) plus ¼-inch worth of threads at the double density of 40 (=10) for a total of 15 + 10, or 25 threads. The middle 10 spaces each have the standard density number of threads (20).

And finally, if the density is intentionally varied to achieve textural vertical stripes, it is best to predetermine the density inch by inch. It is important to remember that you are facing the back of the loom, since the thread sequence will effectively reverse upon moving to the front of the loom. The desired sequence should be spread in the raddle so it will be visually correct from the front of the loom, where it will become woven cloth. (Note: If the warp plan is written so it is correct when viewed from the front of the loom, when raddling at the back of the loom, look at the plan upside down.)

To prevent yarns from escaping their assigned slots, the raddle spaces should be closed off either by wrapping a cord or overlapping stretched rubber bands around consecutive tops of the raddle's vertical dividers.

STRAIGHTENING THE YARNS
Once the threads have been distributed in the raddle, you can begin the somewhat tedious task of straight-

ening the yarns (Fig. 5-6). This process if facilitated by introducing a gentle tension to the warp threads. Move to the front of the loom and, if this has not already been done, divide the warp into smaller groups 3 to 4 inches in width. Pull each of these warp groups along the straightest path possible between the back and front beams by passing through the harnesses and beater. To make this possible, remove the reed from the beater and bunch the heddles together and out of the way. Tie each warp group to the front beam in pretzel fashion (Fig. 5-7). Then return to the back of

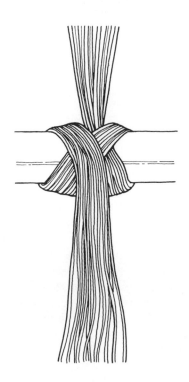

5-7. Pretzel tie

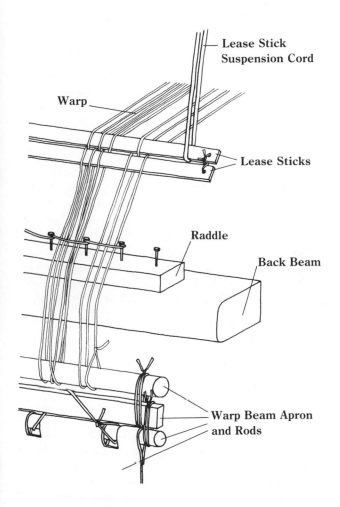

5-6. "Back to front": basic set-up (showing first three threads straightened)

the loom and, starting at one edge of the *X*, follow the course of the first thread back until it meets the warp rod. This first thread should end in a tied loop; pull the loop from the tangle, straightening the entire course of the thread. Return to the *X*, select the next thread, follow its course back to the warp rod, pull to straighten, and continue following the thread (now functionally the next thread in the sequence) back to the *X*. Repeat these steps with each thread across the width of the warp. *(Note:* When a warping paddle has been used to wind the warp, the threads cannot be straightened in this manner. One-inch groups of warp threads should be cut, passed around the warp rod, split in approximate halves, and the halves brought forward and tied above the warp in the same manner as the warp is later tied to the cloth apron rod in preparation for weaving—see Fig. 5-11. The only difference is that the ties should be simple square knots with the shortest tails possible.)

SECURING THE WARP ROD

When all the yarns have been straightened, bind the warp and apron rods together with strong ties (encircling both rods several times) placed at 3- to 4-inch intervals.

The warp is then ready for beaming.

ONE-PERSON BEAMING (ANY WIDTH WARP)

Starting at the back of the loom, move the lease sticks, (gently seesawing them) as far forward against the castle as possible, and undo false knots as you go along. A false knot is nothing more than a catch or tangle; yarn can never form a true, nonslip knot without having at least one loose end. These false knots impede the forward movement of the lease sticks, sometimes causing the sticks to bend. They look as though the warp yarns have reached their limit and are wound around the back lease stick. By simply following these threads back to where they are caught and separating them, you can eliminate the false knot.

Next, move to the front of the loom. (Note: At this point it is advisable to bury cuff buttons by rolling sleeves up and to take off watches and any protruding jewelry.) Beginning at one side, unwrap a pretzel, remove and discard the warp ties, and finger-comb any tangles until they are approximately 1 foot forward of the breast beam. Potential for future false knots can be reduced by inserting one or two fingers in the top lease stick's shed and pulling these fingers forward to separate the yarns. When all the snarls are out, tension the warp group by tugging, and firmly rewrap the straightened group around the breast beam in a pretzel. Repeat this procedure with each warp group across the width of the warp (Fig. 5-8).

After the last group has been straightened and pretzel-tied, go back and tug on the tail of the first warp group. With one hand, lean on the just-tightened pretzel and pull the next group's tail with the other. Repeat this step, in turn, with each warp group. This simultaneous lean/tug with abutting groups corrects tension discrepancies between the groups.

Once the warp is uniformly tensioned, return to the back of the loom and slowly crank the warp onto the warp beam (after removing the temporary ties that suspended the warp and apron rods). Winding should

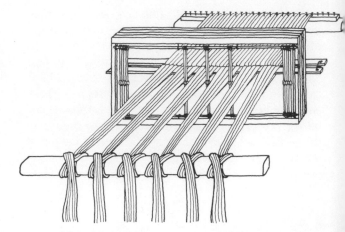

5-8. "Back to front": yarns readied for beaming

meet with some initial resistance. Wear on the warp beam ratchet—and on the person winding—can be minimized by holding the crank handle so it will not unwind and releasing the brake, generally by either stepping on or weighting it, and then silently (without ratchet clicks) beaming. The warp should be winding on in a uniform plane; no individual threads should be shifting in their relationships to one another. When the lease sticks stop moving in unison with the warp and the warp threads start slipping through them, the beaming should stop and the brake be reactivated. At this point, the tension needs to be readjusted.

Again, gently rock the lease sticks forward, release false knots, and resume the finger-combing, straightening, and retying at the front of the loom.

WARP STICKS OR PAPER

Upon returning to the back of the loom, check the wound-on warp to see that each layer is beaming smoothly. These layers should be kept separate, either by beaming in a continuous layer of paper or by inserting warp sticks once or twice per revolution. If paper is used, it should be heavy, without wrinkles, wider than the width of the warp, and not be allowed to wind on crookedly. Heavy brown kraft paper would be suitable. Warp sticks can be made of either wood or metal and should be relatively thin, smooth, and longer than the warp's width.

Continued maintenance of separate layers is fundamental to achieving a consistent tension. As each warp layer is wound on, it effectively increases the circumference of the warp beam for the next layer. Without separation, individual threads will beam inconsistently by switching layers, acting like racers cutting to the inside track.

If the numerous cords joining the warp and apron rods are bulky, they can also create the same uneven beam effect. Rubber-band-hinged warp sticks can be laid in to cover over the cord-formed lumps.

When everything has been checked, and either warp sticks or paper have been added as necessary, the beaming continues until the lease sticks again stop moving. The whole sequence is basically repeated until the warp is almost fully beamed. Upon nearing the end, the unbeamed warp groups become too short to pretzel-tie securely around the breast beam; they are then tied around the lower cross-bar of the beater as it rests against the castle. When the end of the warp no longer reaches the breast beam, the beaming is considered finished.

TWO-PERSON BEAMING (NARROW WARPS)
With two people to share the work of tensioning and beaming, the process is both less tedious and much faster to complete. One person is stationed at the back of the loom while the other is at the front. The person at the back moves the lease sticks forward, checks for and eliminates catches before they become false knots, turns the crank on the warp beam, and inserts either warp sticks or paper as needed. The person at the front finger-combs the yarns to straighten them and holds them under tension with clawed fingers. Both people work in tandem: First they straighten and then the front person tensions while the back person beams. (Again, wear on the warp beam ratchet and on both parties can be reduced if the front person steps on the brake to release it while beaming is in progress.)

However, this method of hand-tensioning is only appropriate in cases where the warp is relatively narrow and can be fully and evenly gripped by the person at the front: Both hands can fan and grip with approximately the same tension, although caution must be exercised not to let the stronger hand rule. When the warp width is increased, the tensioning capability

of two hands is reduced. Adding another pair of hands only compounds the problem. It is extremely difficult, if not virtually impossible, to ascertain when the tension is equalized between different people. Therefore, on wide warps, the one-person method should be used.

Threading
LOGISTICS
The only way to comfortably thread the heddles on a large floor loom is to move the breast beam out of the way, remove the upper cross-piece of the beater (the reed has already been removed), and sit on a low stool so that your eye height and heddle-eye height are approximately the same. With small floor looms and table looms, no changes are necessary.

READING THE THREADING DRAFT
The threading pattern sets forth the sequence for warp end attachment, via heddles, to the harnesses. Threading patterns can be communicated either diagrammatically by a threading draft or in list form. In either case, the numbers referred to indicate specific harnesses; these are traditionally numbered with the first harness being the one closest to the front of the loom.

A threading draft can be viewed as an overhead depiction of the numbered harness shafts (shown stacked horizontally) with the warp ends ticked off (one per vertical line), indicating the place and sequence of their attachment to each harness.

When a threading pattern is given in list form, the numbers indicate on which harness each successive thread is attached. For example, a basic 4-harness point twill pattern can be drafted as in Figure 5-9, or it can be listed as follows: $1 - 2 - 3 - 4 - 3 - 2$. Only the basic sequence of the pattern is given; the final 1 is not listed in order to avoid confusion when the pattern is repeated.

5-9. Threading draft (point twill)

HEDDLE CHECK

Before threading, a careful check should be made to see that the requisite number of heddles called for in the threading draft are placed on the harnesses where they will be needed. With all looms, it is difficult to place additional heddles on harnesses once the threading has begun. In looms where the vertical movement of the harnesses is controlled by slots in the castle frame, it is nearly impossible.

The heddles of a counterbalance loom should be balanced left and right of center within each harness frame. This need be done only once—the central two heddles on each harness can be tagged and the total count recorded. The needed heddles can be counted out from the center and the unneeded extras pushed aside. Where the full width of the harness frame is being used, the heddles that will not be used can be evenly distributed between the threaded heddles across the width of the harness frame.

Additionally, the number of heddles used in counterbalance looms should be the same on all harnesses. There is a widespread belief that counterbalance looms are unsuitable for weaves in which three harnesses are pitted against one. This is probably true where there is a significant difference in the number of heddles (thus heddle weight) on the different harnesses. However, if the harnesses are of the same weight, they can be balanced.

The use of a pattern tie-up on the treadles further perpetrates this myth. Counterbalance looms rarely have more than four harnesses, and probably never should. Only direct (one treadle to one harness) tie-ups should be used. Two feet can always step on three treadles and in so doing manually balance the harnesses against each other to achieve a clear shed. Tie-ups prevent an even shed by causing the harnesses to constantly drag against one another.

THREADING THE HEDDLES

Threading can be done either by catching each warp end with a bent or straight heddle hook, or by using the fingers as if repeatedly threading large needles (heddles) with separate threads (warp ends). If a heddle hook is used, its opening should be large enough to catch each end without separating or splitting it.

To begin threading the warp yarns, first cut their ends. This should be done carefully and without tension to keep the yarns from slipping back out of the lease sticks. To further reduce the risk, you can go to the back of the loom for a moment and move the lease stick suspension cords to support the opposite lease stick. This tips the X forward, preventing the threads from falling out, and makes the cross easier to read from the front of the loom.

Returning to a low seat at the front of the loom, thread the warp ends sequentially (according to their order in the X) and individually—one per heddle eye—in the straightest manner possible, following the threading pattern. When you have completed a basic threading sequence, quickly check to see that no mistakes have been made. Then group the threaded ends together by tying them in a loose, long-tailed slip knot (Fig. 5-10). Repeat this process until all the warp ends have been threaded.

SLEYING THE REED

Next, the threads must be pulled through, or sleyed in, the reed. The correspondence between reed size (reed density) and warp density will determine whether a special sleying pattern need be established, and whether the resulting finished fabric will exhibit subtle or pronounced reed marks (see Appendix C).

Generally speaking, the simplest mathematical relationship between reed and warp density is the best.

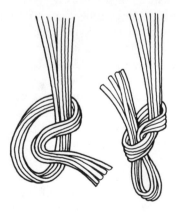

5-10. Slip knot

For example: With a 16 thread per inch warp, use of a 16-dent reed would indicate one warp yarn per reed dent, an 8-dent reed would require 2 per dent, a 4-dent reed would have 4, and a 32-dent reed would mandate leaving every other dent vacant. An unrelated reed size creates textural warp stripes as a result of the necessary unequal distribution of yarns in the dents. The striping can be either regular (i.e., with 16 threads sleyed in a 12-dent reed, an extra thread every third dent would create a consistent rhythm) or not.

Once you have chosen the reed, position and secure it centrally in the beater, and find and mark its center. Central placement helps to keep the beater balanced, which later encourages more uniform weaving. From the reed's center, measure half of the full width of the warp on one side. The last dent to be included in the measuring is the first to be sleyed. Density variations necessitated by a special selvedge treatment would be taken into consideration at this point. It is the grouping in the reed that establishes a double or otherwise different density.

To simplify sleying, move to a higher seat and use either a reed hook (sometimes called an S-hook) or the back side of a bent heddle hook to catch the yarns and draw them through. Each slip knot tail of the threading sequence groups can be pulled as needed to release the threads for sleying. After each 1-inch warp section has been sleyed, this new group of threads should again be tied in a slip knot. This prevents the threads from falling backwards out of the reed and organizes them for the next step.

Tying-Up

Before beginning this step, first spot check the threading to make sure that no errors have passed unnoticed. At this point, both lease sticks and raddle have fulfilled their purposes and should be removed.

Since tying-up is the final step, without inherent future opportunities for readjustments, the harnesses should be checked to see that they are in their dropped or "at rest" positions. Counterbalance and countermarche looms should have all harnesses level; their warp yarns should travel a pure, straight path from back to front beam, through the center of the heddle eyes. If the path should bow, rehang the harnesses to correct the deviation. Once level, counterbalance harnesses may be tied together to ensure that they remain that way throughout warp tying. Jack loom harnesses should cause the warp to noticeably dip, with the warp threads rising to the top of the heddle eyes; if during the tying process the harnesses begin to lift off and "float," weights sufficient to prevent this should be attached and remain in place throughout the weaving.

In attaching the warp to the cloth beam apron rod, straightening and tensioning are again the major concerns. If the cloth rod is simply laced to the apron rod, it is advisable to half-tie the two middle inches of warp first, both outermost inches next, and then systematically work across, half-tying all the others. If cloth and apron rods are firmly fixed in their distance from one another by tied cords, half-tying can begin at one edge and continue straight across. In either case, the procedure is the same for each inch: pull the slip knot tail, freeing the yarn group; quickly yank the yarns to straighten their course through the heddles and finger-comb them to remove tangles; then divide the group roughly in half, draw it forward, pass it around the cloth rod, and bring the ends to the surface and half-tie them as you would begin tying a bow (Fig. 5-11).

After all the inches have been attached in this way, the retensioning begins. Starting with the first inch on one side, grip the tails and pull the yarns horizontally, gently tightening the half-tie. The point of friction should be at the yarn edge passing around the rod, not at the half-knot. (Strong but brittle yarns can break off at the knot if the pull is vertical, focusing the strain there.) This activity is continued sequentially across the warp.

When this is finished, test the tension by firmly patting the warp with a spread palm. The reading of the test will be clearer from the back of the loom, where the warp plane is deeper. If there are differences in the warp's buoyancy, the entire process should be repeated. Spot tensioning yields poor results, takes much longer, and should be avoided. When satisfied that the tension is uniform, generally after two to three com-

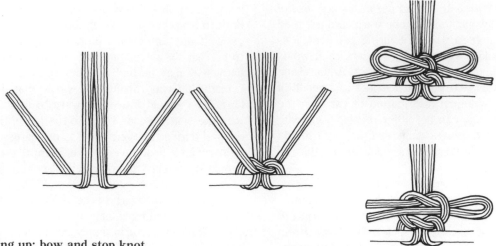

5-11. Tying up: bow and stop knot

plete passes, tie either bows or stop knots without any further adjustments.

Now the weaving can begin.

"FRONT TO BACK"

Threading

RECORDING THE X

The process begins with inserting either a much longer X-cord or lease sticks following each side of the X exactly. Since there is more friction between threads than between threads and wood (lease sticks), the risk of warp threads' slipping out of the lease is reduced if you use the X-cord. On the other hand, the X is more easily seen when maintained by lease sticks. If you use lease sticks, keep them parallel and about ½ inch apart, and secure them at each end with separate ties following a figure-8 path. To make a figure-8, pass the same cord end through the hole of each lease stick, going in the same direction, and then close the cord by tying its ends.

Check the X to see that it has been correctly recorded, and then remove the original, shorter X-ties and retie them tightly around each warp group at a distance approximately half way between the X and the short end of the warp. After this, cut the warp

loop ends. The chokelike retying is a precaution against the warp threads' slipping out from the lease when their ends are severed. These ties can remain fastened throughout the sleying process and each thread separately pulled from the bundle as needed.

SLEYING THE REED

The first task is to sley the warp threads in the reed. This can be accomplished in a number of ways, depending on the reed's position. The reed can (1) be moved to a table and secured in an upright position; (2) be removed from the beater and suspended horizontally between the beater and front beam by resting the reed's ends on lary sticks (Fig. 5-12)—parallel sticks spanning the length between front and back beams—in which case, it is advisable to secure both ends of the reed to each lary stick and tie the lary sticks to both beams; or (3) remain in the beater, with the beater temporarily tied in an upright position approximately 12 inches away from the castle.

The desired effect should determine the size of the reed. Uniform results will be achieved by using a reed in which there is a direct relationship between the number of dents per inch and warp density. For example, 15 ends per inch can be spread evenly in a 5-, 10-, or 15-dent reed, whereas using a 12-dent reed will require uneven distribution, and a 16-dent reed

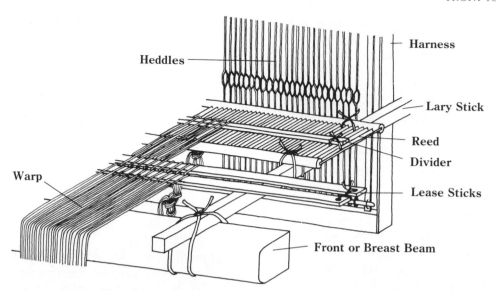

5-12. "Front to back": set-up using lary sticks

will necessitate skipping a dent, thereby causing a pronounced reed mark (see Appendix C). In "front to back" beaming, it is important to minimize potential tension differences between threads during the actual beaming process. Since the reed plays an important role in tensioning the threads, uneven sleying should be avoided because of the increased friction-causing strain on those threads.

Since it will be centered on the loom, the warp should be sleyed centrally in the reed. To do this, determine the reed's center and, from that point, measure a distance that is half of the warp's intended width. The last dent included in the measure will be the first to be sleyed. Sley the ends in the order maintained by the lease sticks or lease cord. The warp end whose sideways movement within the X is unencumbered by any other end is the next in the sequence.

The challenge in sleying the reed is in the maintenance of the X. If the warp and reed densities are the same, then straightforward single sleying will maintain the threads in their correct order. However, if there is a discrepancy—caused by a selvedge treatment, or double, triple, or more sleying — then some system must be instituted to transfer the X from one side of the reed to the other. With double sleying, a stick or

taut cord that laterally divides the reed can be tied in place, and the warp ends can be separated within each dent by systematically sleying above and below this divider. With triple or more sleying, the simplest solution is to place or suspend tied lease sticks on the other side of the reed, either on the table, or between beater and castle, and re-create the X with each warp end. To prevent threads from accidentally slipping backwards and out of dent, use a slip knot with a long tail (Fig. 5-13) to temporarily tie off 1-inch sections. Secure all the warp ends in this manner before moving the reed.

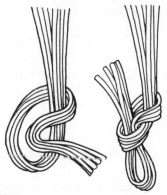

5-13. Slip knot

After all the ends have been sleyed, reposition the reed in the beater (with lary sticks removed) so that these ends are facing the heddles. The bulk of the warp remains forward of the breast beam. If the X has been transferred to new lease sticks, these should be suspended evenly from the castle at heddle-eye height, between the reed and harnesses.

LOGISTICS

The only logical way to undertake the next step—the threading of the heddles—is to position yourself between the castle and the back beam so you are both close to and eye-to-eye with the heddles in the harnesses. With folding looms, the back beam can generally be unhooked and hinged backwards, allowing room for a low stool and easy, comfortable access to the heddles. Rigid construction looms usually require the complete removal of both back and warp beams, generally easily done by simply removing the constructing pegs. No change is necessary when using table or very small floor looms, where access to the heddles over the back beam is no less awkward than access would be from over the front beam.

READING THE THREADING DRAFT

Presented either diagrammatically as a threading draft or in list form, the threading pattern indicates the sequence for warp end attachment, via heddles, to the harnesses. Following either format, start with one and count off the total number of harnesses required for the pattern. The standard diagrammatic notation can be viewed as an overhead depiction showing the numbered harness shafts stacked vertically, and the warp ends marked (one per vertical line) in the order of their attachment to each harness. Because the first harness is traditionally the one closest to the front of the loom, in threading from the back, the diagram should be inverted (Fig. 5-14). The arrangement of harnesses, when viewed this way, mimics the reoriented overhead view experienced by the weaver and places the number one harness in the farthest away position.

When a threading pattern is given in list form, the numbers refer to the harnesses, and the sequence in

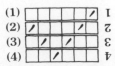

5-14. Threading draft (point twill)

which they appear indicates on which harnesses each successive thread should be placed. A 4-harness point twill could be listed as: 1 – 2 – 3 – 4 – 3 – 2. The final 1 is not listed in order to prevent its repetition when the sequence is repeated.

HEDDLE CHECK

Before threading the heddles, count them to ensure that those required by the threading pattern are already located on the harnesses where they will be needed. Once threading has begun, it is extremely difficult to alter the number of heddles on harnesses, particularly in looms where harness change is guided by tracks on the inside of the castle frame.

Use of a counterbalance loom requires some additional considerations. For this loom to operate smoothly, the heddles must be balanced from side to side within each harness frame; if you tag the middle two heddles on each harness and record the total count, you will have to do this only once. The heddles called for in the threading pattern can then be counted from the center, and the extras can be pushed aside or left unthreaded and evenly distributed across the harness (when the harness's full width is being used).

Regardless of the threading pattern requirements, the number of heddles per harness should be the same in a counterbalance loom. Concentration of heddles on one or two harnesses will cause those harnesses to be considerably heavier and will undermine attempts to achieve a clear shed. Counterbalance looms have long been accused of difficult behavior whenever three harnesses have been worked against one. Unequal heddle weight is a contributing factor, as is a nondirect, or pattern, tie-up of the treadles. Tying more than one harness to a treadle causes the treadle to continually drag on those harnesses. With 4-harness looms (and counterbalance should probably never have more), two feet can always step on three treadles to activate three harnesses. In so doing, the harnesses can be manually balanced to maximize the shed.

THREADING THE HEDDLES

Thread individual yarns, one per heddle eye, in the straightest manner possible, following the dictate of the threading pattern. This can be accomplished with the assistance of either a bent or straight heddle hook, or with the fingers alone. If a heddle hook is used, its notched opening should be sufficiently large to catch the yarn without separating or splitting it.

After threading the complete pattern sequence, check to verify that no mistakes have been made. The threaded ends should then be grouped together and temporarily tied in a long-tailed slip knot. Repeat this process with all the remaining warp ends until all have been threaded and secured.

Beaming
ATTACHING TO THE WARP BEAM

Depending on quantity of slip-knot-tied warp groups, and patience, these groups can be either attached to the warp apron rod as is, or undone and regrouped in 1-inch sections. The procedure for tying each group is as follows: (1) Undo the slip knot and gently finger-comb the warp ends to straighten them and remove major tangles. (2) Unwind enough of the warp beam apron to enable the attached apron rod to be positioned between the back beam and castle. (3) Pull the threads horizontally across the top of the apron rod, passing them first around and then under the rod (Fig. 5-15). (4) Split the group into approximate halves and pull the ends to the surface. Tie these in square knots with the shortest tails possible. If the tails are consistently long, either undo and retie them, shortening the apron by turning the warp beam, or cut them.

LOOM CHECK

At this point, it is advisable to make all the harnesses level so that the warp threads will pass through the center of the heddle eyes following an absolutely straight course from front to back beam. In counter-balance and countermarche looms, this is the correct relationship of the harnesses "at rest." Any discrepancies can be corrected by rehanging the harnesses. Counterbalance loom harnesses can be kept level by temporarily tying them together.

The rest position of the jack loom forces the warp's path downward. This dip is critical for attaining a good-size shed. Some jack looms have built-in mechanisms that elevate the harnesses for threading convenience. With looms that do not, you have two choices: jerry-rig a solution, or leave the harnesses dropped and take your chances. The risk in leaving the harnesses lowered is that when the warp threads are tensioned for winding, they will be straining against the upper edges of all the heddle eyes. This friction could be deadly to fragile or texturally variable yarns. A close watch and sensitized touch are imperative if risk threads are to be identified and trouble averted.

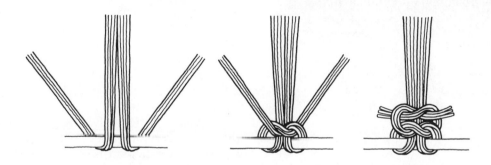

5-15. Tie-up with short-tailed square knots

TWO-PERSON BEAMING

To prepare the yarns for beaming, move to the front of the loom and remove lease sticks, or lease cord, and any temporary sorting devices (laterally tied stick or cord, and so on) from the warp. Since threading has been completed, these are no longer necessary. Remove watches and jewelry, and roll cuff buttons out of the way in order to keep these potential obstructions from catching and breaking threads.

To begin beaming, undo the warp chokes to clear the warp plane as far as 2 to 3 feet forward of the breast beam. Alternately yank and finger-comb the yarns to eliminate all tangles and to realign the threads. With a second person ready at the back of the loom to do the actual cranking, divide the full warp in half and, with clawed fingers and equalized tension, grip each fan-shaped half below the breast beam, pulling the yarns over and against the forward edge of the beam (Fig. 5-16). Then have the second person begin winding. To reduce wear on the warp beam ratchet, the person at the front should release the brake during beaming by stepping on the brake pedal.

As the beaming progresses, the front person's hands should be drawn along with the warp. As soon as the tension feels the least bit reduced or irregular, the beaming should stop. Finger-combing and tensioning should then be repeated before beaming resumes.

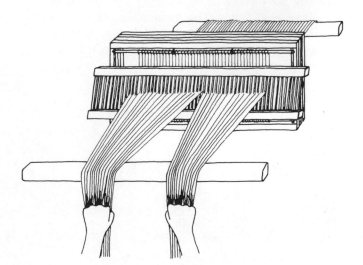

5-16. "Front to back": beaming set-up

WARP STICKS OR PAPER

With each complete revolution of the beam, the warp plane forms separate, spiraling layers. To keep these layers separate, either insert warp sticks, once or twice per revolution, or beam in a continuous layer of paper. These are necessary to offset the yarn's natural inclination to beam unevenly, with threads changing layers and finding different and shorter routes.

Warp sticks are flat smooth sticks that are longer than the warp's width and slightly shorter than the beam. When paper, such as brown kraft paper, is used, it should be relatively heavy, wrinkle-free, and also wider than the warp and narrower than the beam; make sure it does not wind on crookedly.

Use of either begins after the first warp layer has been wound. If the cord connections between warp and apron rods are bulky, several warp sticks can be hinged together with rubber bands and laid in to smooth over the cord-induced unevenness.

The beaming process should be interrupted as needed to allow the person at the back of the loom to insert either warp sticks or paper. The warp is considered fully beamed when the uncut ends at the front of the loom no longer touch the breast beam.

Tying-Up

Tying-up is the final step before actual weaving can begin. In preparation, the harnesses should all be returned to their rest positions. No change will be necessary with counterbalance or countermarche looms; the harnesses on jack looms should all be allowed to sink. If the jack loom harnesses start to rise and "float" during tying, add weights to return them to their correct, lowered positions. These weights should remain attached throughout weaving.

At this point, cut the ends of the warp, being careful not to let them slip out of the reed. Each 1-inch worth of threads should be grouped and temporarily tied with a long-tailed slip knot.

The manner in which the cloth and apron rods are attached to each other determines the sequence in which the separate warp inches will be attached to the cloth rod. If the two rods are laced together, attach the two middle inches first, both outer-edge inches

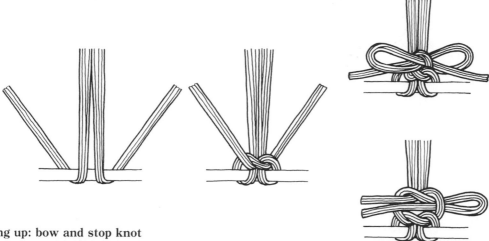

5-17. Tying up: bow and stop knot

next, and then, systematically, all the rest. If the rods are tied a fixed distance apart, tying can begin on one side and continue straight across. Each inch is initially half-tied (as if tying the first half of a bow) in almost the same manner as the threads were originally attached to the warp rod at the back of the loom (Fig. 5-17). The difference is that now the tails should be between 4 and 6 inches long, and the straightening should be more vigorous and include gentle snaps to straighten the yarn's course through the heddles.

When all the inches have been half-tied, retensioning begins. Starting at one edge, pull the tails of the first inch horizontally and gradually, and gently tighten the half-knot. The direction of the pull is important. If horizontal, the strain to individual threads will be negligible because the friction will be spread over the yarn edge passing around the rod. With vertical pulling, enormous stress is focused on the knot, often causing breakage at that point. Tighten each consecutive inch in this manner across the width of the warp.

Test the warp for tension uniformity at the back of the loom, where the warp plane is deeper, by frequent patting. Discovery of differences indicates the need to systematically repeat the tensioning process. Spot tensioning should be avoided—it will take longer and create more problems than it solves.

When the tension is at last even, usually after two to three passes, the remaining part of the stop knot

or bow can be tied; this is done without making any further adjustments.

Weaving can then begin.

SECTIONAL WARPING/BEAMING

Sectional warping/beaming is a self-sufficient, mechanical method that a weaver either chooses to embrace or avoids altogether because of the specificity, quantity, and cost of equipment. It is a method adapted from industry, yet the manner of its use is highly personal. Understanding its basic concept is deceptively simple, but attaining perfect results requires considerable practice and experiential understanding of yarn characteristics.

Because of its inherent speed, the method is often chosen by production weavers, who are continually confronted with very long warps. Time is saved by essentially creating the warp while simultaneously winding it on the beam. The warp's length is thus wound (manually) only once. The technique has the added advantage of warp plan flexibility. Since each warp thread is generated independently, rearrangement of the yarn's sequence—yarn by yarn—is a simple matter.

The primary drawback is the need to develop your own method through trial and error. The differences in available equipment make personal modifications mandatory. Basic difficulties stem from the "hands off" lack of physical involvement with the warp. At first, you can only guess at the relative consistency of the warp's tension. In time, a sixth sense develops, enabling you to make the necessary adjustments to achieve perfect results.

SETUP

Sectional warping and beaming requires the replacement of the loom's ordinary warp beam with a sectional warp beam (Fig. 5-18). This new beam is squarish in cross-section, standardly measures 1 yard around, and has dividing pegs placed at either 1- or 2-inch intervals along the length of each of its four edges. In essence, it combines the characteristics of warping reel, raddle, and beam. Instead of an apron, equal-length cord loops are attached, one per 1- or 2-inch section, across the beam's width.

Begin by taking the chosen warp yarn and winding it in single threads onto separate spools or bobbins. The number of spools required is determined by multiplying the warp density by either one or two—according to the measure of the sections. Extra spools will be required if there is a density increase at the edges because of a selvedge treatment. Thread from

each of these spools will be used in the separate beaming of each section.

Wind either spools with large end caps or bobbins with open ends on an electric winder. (Although it can be done, manual winding should not even be considered. It contradicts the time-saving principle of combined warping and beaming by causing the warp to be essentially hand-wound twice.) The winder basically determines which type of yarn holder can be used. Where there is a choice, spools are preferable because these keep the yarn contained.

The ideal length of the thread that should be wound onto either spool or bobbin is figured by taking the intended warp length and multiplying it by the number of expected repeats. For example: A 12-inch-wide warp contains twelve 1-inch and six 2-inch widths. If the same yarn will appear in each of the sections, then that yarn would be repeating either twelve or six times, respectively. If the desired warp length is 20 yards, then the length to be wound on each spool is 12 × 20, or 240 yards, for 1-inch sections and, for 2-inch sections, 6 × 20, or 120 yards. This length can be accurately measured by using a yarn counter. Whether the basic spool length determined in this manner will be enough depends on how you figure the beamed length (in any case, some extra for leeway should be

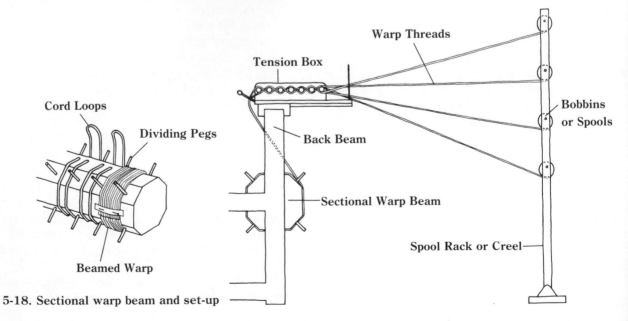

5-18. Sectional warp beam and set-up

figured in). With the winding of each successive layer, the beam's circumference grows. Hence, simple counting of twenty complete revolutions will beam on considerably more than 20 yards. Use of a yarn counter, or separate beaming of a premeasured guide thread, helps in making a more accurate assessment of the beamed length. If you choose to count, make this procedure easier by marking all the dividing pegs on one edge in some manner.

When the correct number of bobbins or spools have been wound, set these into a spool rack, or creel, in the same order as their yarns will later be beamed. Spool racks with independent removable shafts make this task simple. They further facilitate changing the bobbins' order if the yarn sequence varies from section to section.

If bobbins are used, string double cords vertically on the creel and run them down the centers of each bobbin column (Fig. 5-19). Draw the warp yarns between these cords on their way to being threaded in the tension box. The double cords function by pulling the yarns toward the bobbins' centers, reducing the

likelihood that these threads will unwind off the bobbins' ends and subsequently bind.

Next, move the spool rack into position—a minimum of 5 feet away from, and parallel to, the back beam. This distance, in a sense, homogenizes the different angles of the threads' course between the bobbins and tensioner. This equalization helps considerably in the later beaming of a consistent tension.

TENSION BOX/YARN COUNTER
Tension boxes vary considerably. They all function in the same general way, but the exact method for their use differs markedly. Because of this, descriptions will be given for two different models. The steps offered are open to revision, simplification, and elimination as you see fit.

Tensioner #1 (Fig. 5-20) contains a plate with ordered holes at the back of the box, between 5 and 7 immovable tensioning pegs in the middle, and a reed at the front. Tensioner #2 (Fig. 5-20) has two reeds, one at each end, and only three pegs: the outer two fixed, and the central one adjustable.

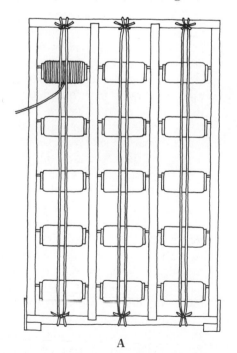

A

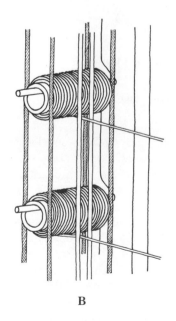

B

5-19. Spool rack (creel) with bobbins and double cords

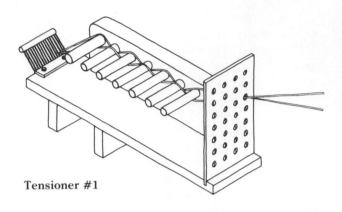

Tensioner #1

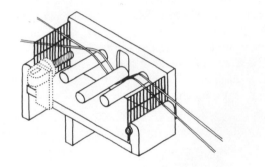

Tensioner #2 (with Yarn Counter)

5-20. Tension boxes: two versions

The plate in tensioner #1 does not change. However, the reed or reeds in both do. These should relate as closely as possible to the warp density. For example: If the warp has 24 threads to the inch, a 24- or 12-dent reed (a 1:1 or 2:1 correspondence) would be best with either tensioner. In tensioner #1, an 8- or 6-dent reed (3:1 or 4:1 ratio) would be acceptable. A reed that does not directly correspond—for example, a 16- or 10-dent—should not be used with either.

A yarn counter (shown outlined in Figure 5-20) is a separate device with an odometer that records thread yardage. Again, variations exist. Some are designed to be attached to the tension box (as shown), while others are meant to be clamped onto the beam next to it. The easiest ones to use are those with resettable counters.

Either type of tensioner and yarn counter is positioned on (clamped to) the back beam directly above the first section to be wound. Since the warp should be centered on the loom, this spot is determined by finding the beam's midpoint and measuring half of the warp's width from there.

THREADING IN THE TENSION BOX
Pull the yarns, one at a time, through the double cord and thread them, singly or in groups, through the holes in the plate (tensioner #1) or sley them in the reed (tensioner #2). At this point, the thread's course changes considerably depending on the tensioner being used.

(Note: As alluded to earlier, if the warp is intended to have a selvedge density variation, the first and last inches to be beamed will have a different quantity of threads. The additional threads should be sleyed in all of the tensioner's reeds on the side where they will be needed. For example, the left-hand selvedge—as judged from the back of the loom, facing front—of a 16-thread per inch warp in a 16-dent reed, with ¾ inch of normal density and ¼ inch of double density, would be sleyed in the following manner: From left to right, the first ¼ inch, or 4-dents, would each have 2 threads, and the remaining ¾ inch, or 12 dents, would be sleyed singly; for the right-hand selvedge, the sequence would exactly reverse—first single sleying 12 dents, and then double sleying 4.)

In the first, fixed-peg tension box, alternate yarns can pursue the opposite slalom course through the pegs and then be sleyed in the reed. This alternating slalom creates a series of crosses. When all the yarns for the full 1- or 2-inch section have been thus threaded (one thread can be pulled across the yarn counter's measuring wheel), the warp ends can be drawn a short distance ahead of the tension box (toward the front of the loom) and tied together with an overhand knot.

In the adjustable peg tensioner, the yarns travel through the reed, take the same over/under/over route, all the yarns passing under the central adjustable peg and then continuing out the second reed towards the front of the loom. With this tensioner, it is best to use reeds that have a 1:2 relationship with the warp density. A horizontal divider should be tied across both reeds, and the threads should be systematically sleyed above and below. This will divide the yarns, producing one shed. (If using a yarn counter, place one thread over its measuring wheel.) Tie all the yarns with an overhand knot.

In both cases, the group of yarns are attached to the cord loop apron belonging to the section to be beamed. This is done by making a lark's head lasso with the end of the cord loop. Insert the overhand knot and pull the lark's head tight, catching and securing the warp ends.

The threads are now ready for beaming.

BEAMING/PACKING
After checking to see that all yarns are in place (if you are using a yarn counter, set it at zero at this point) you can begin winding. For the best results, beaming should be fairly fast and smooth. To guarantee that the threads fall within the right section, on looms with inverted U-shaped dividers, snap on four sets of warp guards framing the section to be beamed, thus funneling the yarns to the correct slot (Fig. 5-21). To minimize wear on the warp beam ratchet, release the brake during beaming.

The use of packing is a personal choice—some weavers swear by it and others feel it is unnecessary. (Most agree that with 1-inch sectional beams, packing should not be used.) Packing is designed to fit between the sectional beam's dividers. It can be made of cardboard, wood, plastic, or thin metal and should look like one of the shapes shown in Figure 5-21. If you choose to use packing, interrupt beaming every 2 to 4 yards to allow for its insertion. Its exact location should be carefully noted and faithfully observed from section to section if the warp tension is to unwind uniformly.

SECURING THE ENDS
When the desired length has been reached, beaming stops, and the warp ends are secured in one of the following ways.

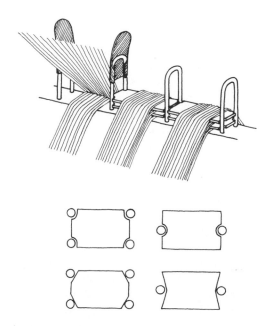

5-21. Warp guards and packing shapes

The standard, easiest, but not necessarily most accurate, method is to flatly tape around the 1- or 2-inch plane of threads; cut them straight across (just above the tape, on the tension box side); reknot the tension box threads to ready them for the next section; and then pin the cut group through the tape to the underlying layer of beamed threads (see Fig. 5-18). It is important to make sure that all is smooth and that the group is not twisted. With 1-inch sectional beams, the damage that can be expected from slightly confusing the order of the threads is fairly minimal. Although stating this is clearly heretical, the simplicity and speed of this technique make it worth considering. The cross-over problems are far more serious in 2-inch sectional widths.

A more time-consuming, exact method involves instituting an *X*. With either tension box method described, one shed has been defined. This can be recorded by inserting either a long or short cord that is immediately distinguishable from the warp. Raise the alternate shed by carefully and sequentially finger-picking through. If a long cord—longer than twice the width of the warp—is used, it should be folded in half at the selvedge edge, and the second half drawn through the new (second) shed. Tie its ends with a large but secure bow. With a short cord, the same activity takes place, but the tails are shorter. After the *X* has been secured, hold all the yarns flat and tape the warp between the *X* and the tension box, cut, tie off the other ends (those still threaded through the tension box), and pin the taped ends in the same manner as described above.

The advantage to using the longer cord is that it can be untied, used to record the *X* in each consecutive section, and then retied. This long cord thus becomes an equivalent to lease sticks, maintaining not only the *X*, but also the order of the groups.

The short cord, on the other hand, enables each section to be totally independent. If adjacent sections are not beamed in order, only use of a shorter cord makes sense. If a color pattern is repeating several sections over, it would be easiest to beam that repeat before rearranging the order of the threads in the tension box.

Basically, each section is beamed and secured as described, before proceeding to the next section. The sequence in which the sections are beamed is, however, another open question, again with divergent opinion.

TENSION

The tension of the yarn coming off the spools changes as the spools lose yarn. With rapidly decreasing circumferences, the spools unwind faster and with less drag. Tensioner #1 is nonadjustable and ignores this fact—figuring that the number of crosses in the box will adequately compensate. The movable peg in tensioner #2 is gradually adjusted downwards to increase the tension on the yarns and offset the expected tension loss.

Given this variable state of affairs, some weavers feel that beaming should be staggered, so differences will not follow a steady progression from selvedge to selvedge. Whether this strategy will really neutralize variable tension is questionable. It is probably better to do whatever is possible to maintain the most uniform

tension, whatever the spool speed. Increasing the distance of the creel from the back beam may be helpful, as may be tying cords on the creel (parallel to the doubled cords) to hug each side of the bobbins (Fig. 5-19b). The friction from these cords may help to control the bobbins' spin. Then again, you may find that the spool changes do not significantly affect the tension emerging from the tension box.

In short, this is where observation and the development of a sixth sense become crucial. Throughout winding, it is important to keep aware of the relative speed of the bobbins. Any spool or bobbin that noticeably, or audibly, begins to spin faster than the others is probably running short on yarns. It is best for the warp if the yarn does not run out during beaming. Yarns that prematurely end will require a knot (to a new thread) somewhere in the middle of the warp's length. Knots can cause tension problems if they later catch in the heddles or reed and stretch or break. The best solution is to substitute a new spool with more thread before beaming the next section. If, however, due to miscalculation, the yarn does run out, then the knots used should be either square or weaver's knots (Fig. 5-22) and tied as tightly as possible.

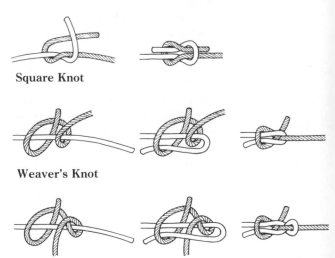

Square Knot

Weaver's Knot

Double Weaver's Knot

5-22. Square and weaver's knots

PREPARATION FOR THREADING

When all the sections have been evenly beamed, the warp must be partially unwound and advanced to allow the yarns enough length to be threaded. The simple technique for doing this varies according to the end-securing system used earlier.

First, the warp groups are unpinned.

With the warp sections that have crosses, insert lease sticks, each following the opposite shed (Fig. 5-23, *A*). Lease stick substitutions for the long *X*-cord are simple and direct; with the shorter cords, make sure that the groups are taken in order and that they remain straight and untwisted. The lease sticks should be kept parallel, spaced approximately ½ inch apart, and their ends tied with cords following a figure-8 path.

With the non-*X*, taped-only groups, sandwich the warp between stacked lease sticks (Fig. 5-23, *B*). Bind the lease sticks intermittently and tie their ends without figure-8s.

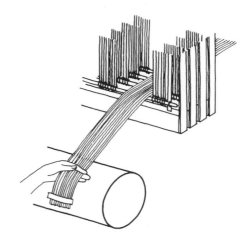

5-24. Set-up for threading of taped-only sections

Release the brake and pull the lease sticks, drawing the yarns, now forming a plane, up and around the back beam. When the lease sticks can touch the back of the castle, suspend them so they hang at heddle-eye height.

Continue unwinding a little at a time, and pull the warp groups separately toward the front of the loom. This effectively moves the lease sticks further back in the warp and away from the taped ends.

When the taped ends reach the breast beam, stop the unwinding. The crossed groups are ready to be threaded normally, but the groups relying on the tape for their order require special handling. Essentially, these tape-ordered groups keep their tapes on. The exact order of their threads is easiest to see if each group is brought forward to the cloth beam as needed and held straight under modest tension (Fig. 5-24). Pull, or cut, each thread individually from the tape just before you are ready to thread it. Afterwards, cut off the taped part of the yarn because oxidation of the tape adhesive can later cause discoloration.

Basic threading and further, more specific instructions can be found by turning to the "Back to Front" section and reading the entries beginning with Threading (page 95).

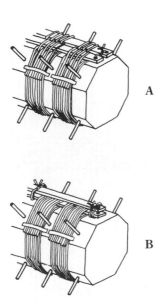

5-23. Advancing the warp

A

B

6 Weaving/Troubleshooting

Actual weaving is at once both straightforward and involved. It is in many ways like driving a motor vehicle: Initially it requires very focused attention, but, with practice, becomes instinctive. In both cases, mechanical decisions—the maneuvering involved in turning a corner, for example—are best handled by trusting physical alertness and skill, and pushing mental thought aside. A few basic principles need only to be reinforced by experience to develop the correct instincts.

AMOUNT OF ARCH

As mentioned frequently in previous chapters, the ratio of warp to weft determines the amount of each element's take-up in the weave. In balanced weave, for example, both elements undulate along their respective routes by roughly equal amounts; in weft-face, the warp is inflexible, and the weft does all the circum-navigating. Because the warp is controlled by the loom in all the weaves, it falls to the weaver to make the necessary accommodations with the weft. If the weft is to assert itself, it will need additional length.

This length is achieved by either arching or angling the weft within the shed (Fig. 6-1). The shape of the arch will vary according to woven structure, weaving width, and yarn character. There is a delicate balance between what is too much, too little, and the correct amount of arch. To establish that you have the right amount, examine the weaving's edges. Pushing the weft in place (Fig. 6-2) before forming the arch can help to regulate the edge.

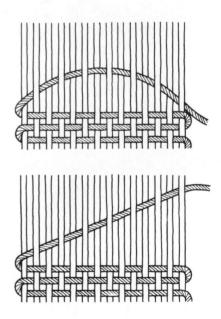

6-1. Arching/angling the weft through the shed

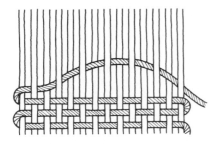

6-2. Fixing the weft's placement at the weaving's edge

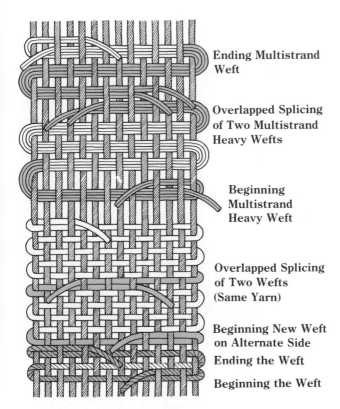

Ending Multistrand Weft

Overlapped Splicing of Two Multistrand Heavy Wefts

Beginning Multistrand Heavy Weft

Overlapped Splicing of Two Wefts (Same Yarn)

Beginning New Weft on Alternate Side

Ending the Weft

Beginning the Weft

6-3. Beginning, ending, and overlapping the weft

BEGINNING AND ENDING WEFTS

One of the main virtues of the weft is its independence—its ability to come and go at will. The simple technique for disguising these entries and exits is to overlap the new yarn with the old (Fig. 6-3). If this is done within the same shed, the overlap will be nearly invisible. An overlap of an inch is generally sufficient—the friction of the compressed yarns will prevent later separation. With frequent color changes, beginning and ending sides should be alternated to reduce the risk of weft-pile-up. Multiple-strand wefts can be overlapped by staggering their ends over a greater length.

The yarn's actual ends should be left exposed on either the front or back face of the fabric. After several more rows of weaving have been completed and danger of accidental cutting of the raised warp has passed (see Fig. 6-10), the ends can be clipped flush to the surface.

The one exception to this method of reweaving the weft ends into the cloth should be made in weft-face weaving. A doubled weft thickness would prevent even packing down of subsequent rows. Weft-face weft ends should therefore be darned in along the warp after the weaving has been removed from the loom.

POSTURE

Weaving is thought to be notoriously bad for the back, primarily because poor posture, poor habits, and the wrong seating height focus enormous strain there.

To reduce strain, make sure your posture is flexibly upright—neither locked nor hunched—with your shoulders parallel to the harnesses. (Hunching is by far the most common, mistakenly adopted pose—perhaps because it enables a closer view of the web. Continual close inspection of this sort is unnecessary.) You should sit directly centered in front of the loom.

Stool or bench height (for floor looms) should be such that your knees drop below your hips and that (for all looms) your elbows lean comfortably on the breast beam. Your knees need to be lower than your hips so that the weight necessary for bearing down on the treadles (to activate the harnesses) can easily be transmitted through them. This hip/knee relationship is contrary to the standard orthopedic advice for sitting, but that recommendation—to elevate the knees—is for sitting only and will actually induce lower back strain when you operate a floor loom. The situation is comparable to riding a bicycle versus peddling a go-cart.

Wherever possible, all physical movements should be either balanced or alternated. Putting weight on both feet simultaneously is easier and less exhausting. Two feet will not need to push as hard as one will, and their combined weight will naturally be heavier. In addition, constant shifting of the hips will be avoided.

Both you and your weaving will benefit from pulling the beater at its exact center and with alternate arms. You will be rhythmically twisting, while the beater is consistently squared with the web. With the whole body involved equally, there is less tendency to overwork one side and cause cramping.

In weaving yardage, developing the simplest and smoothest rhythm will automatically encourage uniformity and increase production speed. However, frequent time out to get up and stretch should be mandatory with all weaving. The time lost is more than compensated for by the improvement in stamina.

THREADING ERRORS

Generally speaking, you have probably checked and counterchecked both the heddles and the reed enough times that threading errors rarely last long enough to be made visible. Yet on occasion, they do happen (letters correspond to those shown in Fig. 6-4): *(A)* a thread is drawn through the heddle incorrectly; *(B)* the same harness is mistaken for its neighbor; *(C)* a dent is missed; *(D)* two threads are misdented; or *(E)* a thread in the sequence is forgotten. These types of errors should be clear in the *heading*—the temporary weaving that bridges between the knots and the uniform cloth—but in this photograph they are shown continuing into the weaving for the sake of clarity. *(Note:* The heading is not generally considered part of the fabric. Its depth—the distance necessary for the gradual shifting of the yarns' positions in response to the reed—will be approximately the same, regardless of weft size. Hence, fewer, heavier weft rows will be faster to put in and later to remove.)

IN THE HEDDLES

The *directional misthreading of a heddle* (see *A* in Figure 6-4 and the close-up in Figure 6-5) is visually one of the most subtle mistakes. Upon close inspection, you can see the thread floating above all the other yarns that share the same shed. Closer scrutiny of the woven cloth will reveal the slightly independent character of the yarn in question—it seems a bit straighter and tactily is more taut than its neighbors. This thread is in fact being considerably stressed by friction with the heddle, which causes an increase in tension. In time, over a distance, it will visually become increasingly more aberrant. The constant battle between heddle and yarn will wear the yarn down, increasing the likelihood of breakage. The only solution to this sort of error is to rethread the heddle. But once you become accustomed to threading, you will find that an error of this type will become physically hard to make.

The straight threading error *(B* in Figure 6-4) caused by *choosing the wrong heddle* is fairly blatant: Three yarns are weaving as if they were one. Because of the simple plain weave requirement that adjacent yarns assume opposing positions, with one warp yarn passing over the weft and the next under, it is clear that the middle thread is the misbehaving one. Its presence indicates that the total number of threads required by the threading pattern are in place—so misthreading is the only error. The solution to this problem demands the simple addition of a new heddle. Rather than unthreading and rethreading all the correctly threaded yarns between the site of the error and the selvedge in order to get the new heddle to the place where it is needed, you can tie the traditional string heddle (Fig. 6-5) in place. If metal heddles are being used, an alternative solution is to take an extra heddle, clip (as shown in Figure 6-6) one side of each of the heddle bar openings, and carefully work the heddle onto the heddle bars of the correct harness. With both these solutions, you must be careful to secure the new heddle on heddle bars that are on the same harness.

Forgetting to thread or *omitting a thread in the pattern sequence (E* in Figure 6-4) can either be as subtle as shown, or be made vivid by a pattern threading/treadling. It can be distinguished from the simpler problem of wrong heddle choice by counting and as-

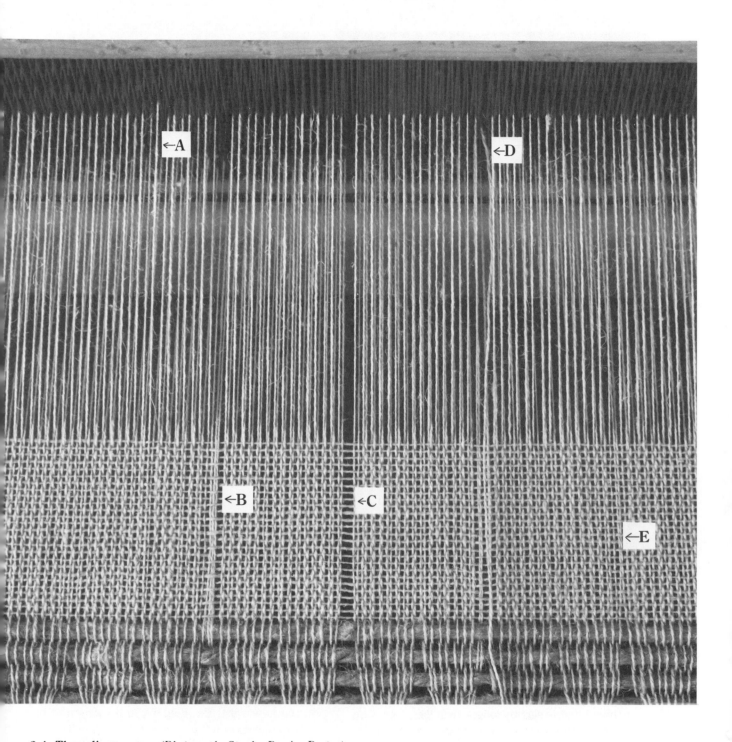

6-4. Threading errors. *(Photograph: Stanley Rowin, Boston)*

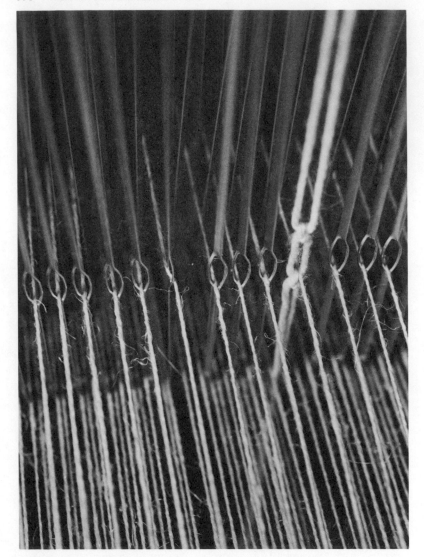

6-6. Metal repair heddle

6-5. Misthreaded heddle and repair (string) heddle.
(Photograph: Stanley Rowin, Boston)

certaining the absence of enough threads to complete the pattern. Its solution requires the addition of both a new heddle and a new yarn, and the resleying of all the threads between the problem site and the edge of the fabric. The new yarn can be added by winding a new thread that is slightly longer than the other warp yarns onto a yarn carrier (the increased length enables the later tying of the new yarn to the warp beam apron rod when it resurfaces toward the end of the weaving); threading one end of the thread through the new heddle, sleying it in the reed, and tying it up in the normal fashion; and suspending the yarn package so it drags off the back beam (Fig. 6-7). If more tension is needed on the new yarn, the holder can be weighted or a heavier one chosen (i.e., a wooden spool, metal pipe). The holder shown has been weighted with four dimes.

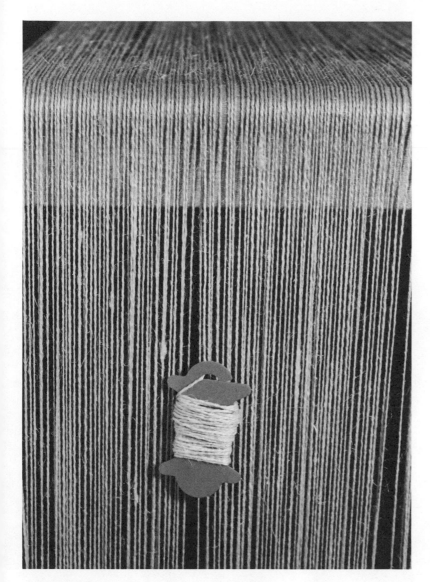

6-7. Addition of a new yarn via yarn holder.
(Photograph: Stanley Rowin, Boston)

IN THE REED

Either *skipping a dent* (C in Figure 6-4) or overcrowding yarns within one (not shown) are glaring errors that require giving in and resleying all the yarns from that point over to the nearest edge. If there are a number of these errors, after resleying, the reed's position can be slightly shifted within the beater to adjust for the new fabric width.

Cross-denting two threads (D in Figure 6-4) causes them to bind with each other and float midshed. A run in the cloth (as shown) can result from the suspension of the threads, preventing one of them from ever becoming part of the lower shed. Initially, the tension of both threads is increased, but because of the noninteraction of one of the threads, that yarn appears to grow and steadily lose tension. After a while, its lackluster character may permit it enough sag that it will temporarily join the lower shed. If this happens, it will weave correctly for a bit, and then the cycle will repeat itself. The problem is remedied by resleying the crossed threads.

TENSION PROBLEMS

If, in weaving, the weft angle slowly goes askew, deviating from the right angle, the warp tension is probably at fault. Uneven tension causes unevenness in the weave. The tension irregularity can be the result of either poor (insufficient or irregular) winding tension during beaming or poorly tied tension at the loom's

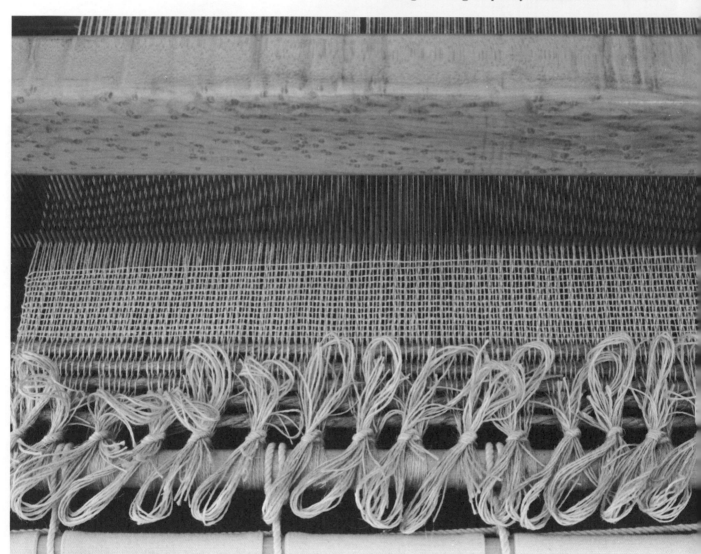

6-8. Tension problems: steadily diminishing tension between selvedges.
(Photograph: Stanley Rowin, Boston)

front. The former case may reveal itself as you finish beaming by the remaining presence of unequal warp lengths. Otherwise, you will discover it by realizing that in tying-up, abnormal amounts of retensioning seem to be necessary, and that this is producing dramatically increasing tyable warp lengths. If heavy paper has been used to keep the warp layers separate, their looseness, which is an indicator of too little winding tension, will be clear—you will hear the sound of the warp layers slipping past each other and feel the yarns spiraling movement around the beam.

The only solution in a case like this is to carefully unwind the full warp's length, drawing it slowly through the heddles and reed, and across the breast beam. The unbeamed length can be chained to condense it during unwinding. When all has been unwound, the full beaming can be repeated in the same manner as described in chapter 5, Dressing the Loom "Front to Back" (begin with Beaming: Loom Check).

Chances are good, however, that the problem is less ingrained and instead rests with incomplete tensioning when tying the warp to the cloth apron rod.

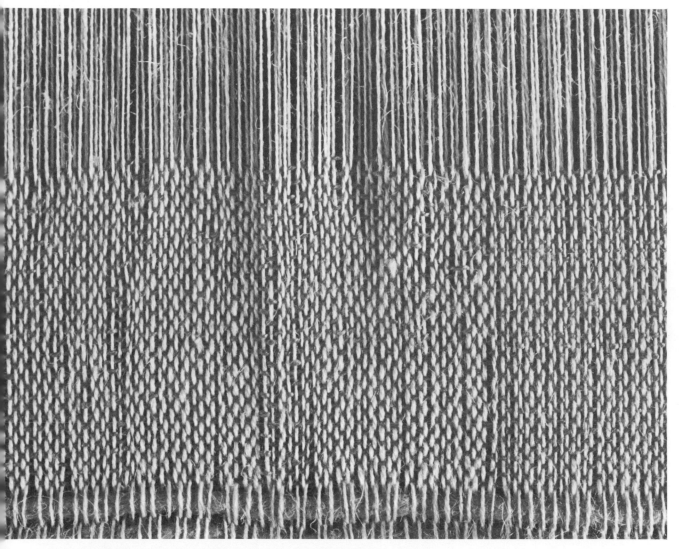

6-9. Tension problems: erratic tension. *(Photograph: Stanley Rowin, Boston)*

If there is increased weft buildup on one side only, that is an indication of steadily diminishing warp tension across the width of the fabric. The tallest side is the one with the slackest tension (Fig. 6-8). (There is one other possible and/or contributing cause for this kind of problem: if the beater is loose, it may be beating crookedly. Continual pulling from only one side will accentuate the angled beat. To remedy this, tighten the beater's bolts. If the problem rests with warpage of the beater's wooden cross-pieces, these should be replaced.) If, however, the weaving plane becomes bumpy and the weft packs down erratically, the fault lies with a thoroughly uneven tension (Fig. 6-9).

If either case, the warp will have to be untied, re-tensioned properly, and retied. It is far better to focus on these problems and delay beginning to correct them than it is to proceed and hope that all will work out. You can practically be guaranteed that tension problems will not be self-correcting. Instead, they have an almost sinister way of magnifying.

Those that for whatever reason develop in the course of the weaving (midway in the fabric, not in the heading) can only be dealt with by *stuffing*—inserting yarn scraps, pieces of paper, and so on, under the loose warp thread (or groups of threads). This will effectively increase the distance that the yarn (or yarns) will have to travel and, hence, compensate for the yarn's slackness. This stopgap remedy should be postponed for as long as possible. As more of the warp length is unwound, the lack of tension problem will increase. If the problem area has been stuffed, it will need increased feeding. You can wind up spending much of your time fudging adjustments at the back of the loom.

If, on the other hand, the tension abnormality is caused by yarns (or yarn) that are too tight, and if there are not too many of them, you can fully correct the problem in a different way. These threads can each be separately cut and treated as if they were broken (see Weaving Problems). The new bridge yarn can then be tied to the correct tension. To more easily disguise these substitute yarns in the finished piece, stagger their cut ends as much as possible.

WEAVING PROBLEMS

If everything else is correct, the only warp difficulties that will occur during weaving are broken threads and arch problems.

BROKEN THREADS

A broken thread can be caused by inherent yarn weakness such as uneven spinning in a single-ply yarn, or fractured threads in a complex novelty yarn; straining and thus weakening conditions in a yarn, due perhaps to knots that continue to catch in either heddle or reed; or accident caused by shuttle collisions with a weak yarn or by cutting.

The two broken ends depicted in Figure 6-10 were victims of cutting —they were severed when the new and old overlapped weft yarns were trimmed. To be safer, the weft ends should not have been cut until the weave had substantially progressed. Weft ends should only be cut with scissors kept parallel to, rather than angled into, the cloth. With any degree of angle, and with sharp scissors especially, the warp can be easily sliced. If the shed is raised, even parallel scissors can readily cut the warp. Had the weave been further along, the flat scissors would not have been able to reach, and cut, the lifted warp yarns.

Of the two cut threads, the one on the left has dropped out of sight, having slipped backwards and out of the reed: it looks like a threading and denting error, which is in essence what the problem has become. The thread on the right has been repaired.

The repair consists of adding a new yarn to temporarily replace the old. This is done by first knotting the ends of both old and new yarns and then drawing the now much longer thread back through the reed and heddle. The knot can then be untied, or cut out, and replaced by a very long looped bow placed a distance behind the heddle. The free end of the thread is drawn across the surface of the cloth, exactly retracing its former course; it is given the same tension as the other threads, and secured by several figure-8 wraps around a T-pin. The sharp end of the pin can then be tucked into the weave to lock the wrapped thread and prevent later scratching of hands and

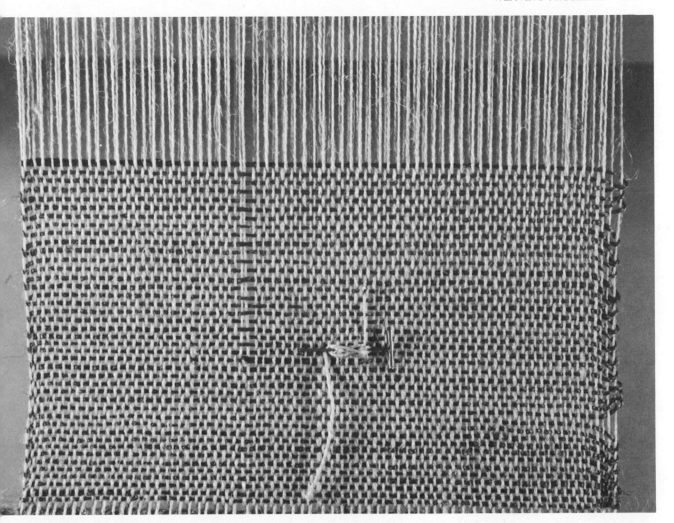

6-10. Weaving problems: too much and too little arch; broken thread.
(Photograph: Stanley Rowin, Boston)

forearms. (You should also be careful that the loom is not scratched when the cloth passes around the front beam. This danger can be easily averted by untucking the pin's point, winding enough length forward that the pin area is beyond the beam, and reinserting the point in the cloth afterwards.)

Weaving proceeds normally until the floppy bow reaches the backside of the heddles. The cloth should be woven to as great a depth as possible, filling the space between breast beam and the reed against the castle. This will ensure that the final steps can be carried out. At this point, the earlier steps are basically reversed, and repeated: The bow is untied, its extreme ends are tied to each other, and the yarn is pulled through the heddle and reed, towards the front of the loom. The ends are again untied, or the knot cut, and the "new" end, which is actually part of the old warp, can be T-pinned to the cloth. The weaving's

6-11. Weaving problems: insufficient arch. *(Photograph: Stanley Rowin, Boston)*

depth enables the warp yarn to be long enough to pin when it reaches the woven cloth.

When the weaving is finished and the fabric has been released from tension and taken off the loom, the T-pins can be removed and the loose warp ends can be sewn alongside the woven warp threads in the cloth, with approximately 1 to 1½ inches of overlap. This is essentially the same as the usual weft splices. If the fabric is to be washed or finished in some other way, all the warp ends should be sewn in first.

ARCH PROBLEMS

In Figure 6-10, the edge at the left has been progressively narrowing due to a lack of arch. Its profile is dented because of recognition of the problem, and consequent compensation to work the weaving back out to its correct width. Just as the problem was a slowly worsening one, its resurrection takes time and length. The yarns under tension will not suddenly change direction of their own accord.

The right-hand selvedge betrays the opposite problem: weaving with too much arch (at least at the very edge). The weft thread can be seen loosely encasing the warp, and the two elements are barely interacting. The warp therefore grows and loses tension. The weft has excess length and so it meanders, sliding down on top of itself and creating an unsatisfactory weft-face weave.

The two edges are juxtaposed within the same weaving and across a fairly narrow width, testifying to the localized natures of these problems. A degree of overtightness is clearly visually preferable to awkward, overly loose, and insubstantial weaving. For some unknown reason, if one is right-handed, the left selvedge tends to be automatically crisper (the reverse is true for left-handed weavers). In the beginning, constant comparisons between the two edges can help to identify the wrong amount of arch.

However, this method also requires checking against the reed. In Figure 6-11, the arch has been steadily reduced, with the result that although the edges look uniform, they have dramatically narrowed. The full width of the fabric has shrunk by nearly 4 dents on each side. Since this is an 8-dent reed, with a warp density of 16 threads per inch, and thus 2 threads per dent, that means a reduction of ½ inch from each selvedge. The condition is thus extreme, yet is simultaneously made subtle by the fact that the warp plane is horizontal and seen receding in space (keystoning because of perspective). This creation of a trapezoidal weaving is not only potentially undesirable (if such a creation is uncontrollable), but is also unhealthy for the reed (you can see how the reed wire has been pulled out of alignment) and, ultimately, disastrous for the warp as well. With time, the steadily increasing friction will abrade the edge yarns until they break.

Furthermore, working out a cinching-in of this sort is extremely difficult. The wider width, as it is slowly created, will tend to buckle, much like a dirndl skirt gathered into a waistband. A temple (shown in Figure 4-3) can be attached to both selvedges, pushed down to spread the edges, and locked in that position to keep them spread. But you should not develop a dependency on a temple—its claws can be damaging to a delicate weaving. It is far better to be self-reliant. Finding the right arch does take patience and discipline, but once the instinct for creating it has been developed, that instinct is dependable.

Appendix A
Burn Test for Fiber Identification

The burning method is given here because it is the simplest test and offers a useful handle with which to narrow your choices in trying to determine the nature of an unknown fiber. Other, more scientific tests are necessary if an absolute determination is to be made.

In general, natural fibers form an ash and synthetics melt. Of the natural fibers, those of plant origin have an inoffensive odor, and those that are animal smell (appropriately) like burning hair. Smell, without burning, can help with some diagnoses: Wool's odor when wet will readily disclose its presence, and both wild silk and jute have their own distinctive scents. With time, the various fibers can be identified by feel, but because fiber blends can be deceptive, the presence of synthetics may be discoverable only by burning.

Fiber	Approaching Flame	In Flame	Removed from Flame	Odor	Ash
Cotton	Scorches; ignites easily	Burns quickly; yellow flame	Continues to burn without melting; afterglow	Burning paper	Small, fluffy gray ash black ash = mercerized
Linen	Scorches; ignites easily	Burns quickly (thick yarns burn more slowly than cotton)	Continues to burn without melting	Burning paper	Small, fluffy gray ash
Wool	Fuses and curls away from flame	Slow, flickering flame; yarn curls	Sometimes self-extinguishing	Burning hair	Crisp dark ash, crumbles easily
Silk	Fuses and curls away from flame	Burns slowly; some melting	Often self-extinguishing	Milder burning hair, or burning feathers	Round black bead, crushes easily
Rayon	Scorches; ignites quickly	Burns quickly; yellow flame	Creeping ember	Burning paper or wood	Light gray and feathery
Nylon	Fuses and shrinks away from flame	Burns slowly with melting	Usually self-extinguishing	Somewhat pungent	Hard, round gray bead
Metallics (pure metals)	Do not burn	Glow red	Harden	None	Original shape
Coated metallics	Fuse and shrink	Melt	Depends on coating	None	Hard bead
Acrylic	Fuses away from flame	Burns rapidly; melts	Continues to burn and melt	Harsh, sharp, bitter	Hard irregular black bead
Polypropylene	Fuses, shrinks, curls away from flame	Burns very slowly; melts	Burns with difficulty	Chemical	Hard round tan bead
Saran	Fuses and shrinks away from flame	Slowly; melts	Self-extinguishing	Sharp, bitter	Hard irregular black bead
Polyester	Fuses and shrinks away from flame	Burns slowly; melts	Usually self-extinguishing	Sharp	Hard black brittle round bead

Appendix B
Warp Length Calculations

LOOM LOSS FACTOR

Basic: approximately 1 yard (92 cm. or for convenience round up to 1 m.)

For deep-castled, multiharness looms (8 or more harnesses): 1 yard + extra castle depth (6 to 8 inches) (1 m. + 10 to 15 cm.)

For small looms (measuring 2 feet—60 cm.—or less between front and back beams): between ⅝ and ⅞ yard (.7m. and .9 m.) (the lower sum for looms with beam spread of 18 inches—43 cm.—or less)

WARP ABSORPTION ALLOWANCE

Length + (length × warp absorption %) + loom loss factor = total warp length

The desired length of the cloth = *length*

Length is multiplied by *warp absorption* % of either 25%, 10%, or 5%, as determined by the weave type:

    25%—warp-face and warp-face balance weaves
    10%—balanced weaved
    10% to 5%—weft-face balanced weave
    0 to 5%—weft-face weave

For the most accuracy, always work with the smallest unit of measuure. It is best to determine the length in inches (or centimeters) but is more convenient (and permissable) to determine it in feet. It will be too inaccurate, and hence should not be determined in yards (or meters). The length can be converted into yards (or meters) later. (It is important that all numbers used in calculations refer to the same unit of measure.)

Example: 16-foot length, warp-face weave, standard loom size
16 + (16 × .25) + 3 = (16 + 4 + 3) = 23 feet or 7⅔ yards total warp length

Appendix C
Warp/Reed Density Distribution Patterns

REED DENSITY (*Dents/Inch*)

WARP DENSITY (*Threads/Inch*)	5	6	8	10	12	15	16	18	20	24
5	1			1/0		1/0/0			1/0/0/0	
6		1	1/1/1/0		1/0		1/0/0			1/0/0/0
8		2/1/1	1	1/1/1/1/0	1/1/0		1/0			1/0/0
10	2	2/2/1	2/1/1/1	1	1/1/1/1/1/0	1/1/0			1/0	
12		2	2/1		1	1/1/1/0	1/1/0	1/1/0		1/0
15	3	3/2		2/1		1			1/1/1/0	
16		3/3/2	2		2/1/1		1		1/1/1/1/0	1/0
20	4	4/3/3	3/2	2	2/2/1	2/1/1	2/1/1/1		1	1/1/1/1/1/0
24		4	3		2		2/1	2/1/1	2/1/1/1/1	1
25	5			3/2		2/2/1			2/1/1/1	
30	6	5	4/4/4/3	3	3/2	2		2/2/1	2/1	2/1/1/1
36		6	5/4		3		3/2/2	2	2/2/2/2/1	2/1
40	8	7/7/6	5	4	4/3/3	3/3/2	3/2		2	2/2/1

Blanks indicate that no regular pattern is possible.

Boxed patterns indicate a strong reed mark every ½ inch.

Underlined patterns indicate reed marks every ¼ inch.

Note: Reed marks will be prominent wherever dents have been skipped, or unequal numbers of threads have been sleyed through them.

Appendix D
Metric Equivalents
Reed Sizes and Warp/Reed Density Distribution Patterns

REED SIZES

Dents/Inch	Dents/Cm.
5	2
8	3
10	4
12	5
15	6
18	7
20	8

REED DENSITY (*Dents/Cm.*)

WARP DENSITY (*Threads/Cm.*)

	2	3	4	5	6	7	8
2	1	1/1/0	1/0		1/0/0		1/0/0/0
3	2/1	1	1/1/1/0		1/0		
4	2	2/1/1	1	1/1/1/1/0	1/1/0		1/0
5	3/2	2/2/1	2/1/1/1	1	1/1/1/1/1/0		
6	3	2	2/1	2/1/1/1/1	1	1/1/1/1/1/1/0	1/1/1/0
7	4/3	3/2/2	2/2/2/1		2/1/1/1/1/1	1	1/1/1/1/1/1/1/0
8	4	3/3/2	2		2/1/1	2/1/1/1/1/1/1	1
9	5/4	3	3/2/2/2	2/2/2/2/1	2/1		2/1/1/1/1/1/1/1
10	5	4/3/3	3/2	2	2/2/1		2/1/1/1
11	6/5	4/4/3	3/3/3/2	3/2/2/2/2	2/2/2/2/2/1		
12	6	4	3		2		2/1
13	7/6	5/4/4	4/3/3/3		3/2/2/2/2/2	2/2/2/2/2/2/1	
14	7	5/5/4	4/3	3/3/3/3/2	3/2/2	2	2/2/2/1
15	8/7	5	4/4/4/3	3	3/2	3/2/2/2/2/2/2	2/2/2/2/2/2/2/1

Note: Reed marks will be prominent wherever dents have been skipped or unequal numbers of threads have been sleyed through them.

Bibliography

Bergman, Ingrid. *Late Nubian Textiles*. Sweden: Berlingska Boktryckeriet Lund, 1975.

Birrell, Verla. *The Textile Arts*. New York: Schocken Books, 1959.

Black, Mary E. *New Key to Weaving*. New York: Macmillan Publishing Co., Inc., 1957.

Boser-Sarivaxévanis, Renée. *Les Tissus de L'Afrique Occidentale*. Basler Beiträge zur Ethnologie Band 13, Pharos-Verlag Hansrudolf Schwabe A G. Bâle, 1972.

Carter, Herbert R. *The Spinning and Twisting of Long Vegetable Fibers*. Philadelphia: J. B. Lippincott Co., 1904.

Collingwood, Peter. *The Techniques of Rug Weaving*. New York: Watson-Guptil Publications, 1969.

Constantine, Mildred, and Larsen, Jack Lenor. *The Art Fabric: Mainstream*. New York: Van Nostrand Reinhold Co., 1981.

Corbman, Bernard P. *Textiles: Fiber to Fabric*. 6th ed. New York: McGraw-Hill Book Company, 1983.

Emery, Irene. *The Primary Structures of Fabrics*. Washington, DC: The Textile Museum, 1966.

Fiske, Patricia L.; Pickering, W. Russell; Yohe, Ralph S., ed. *From the Far West: Carpets and Textiles of Morocco*. Washington, DC: The Textile Museum, 1980.

Groff, Russell E. *Sectional Warping*. McMinneville, OR: Robin and Russ Handweaver's, 1979.

Held, Shirley E. *Weaving: A Handbook for Fiber Craftsmen*. New York: Holt, Rinehart and Winston, Inc., 1973.

Jarvis, P. R. *A Practical Weaving Course*. Manchester and London: Harlequin Press, 1947.

Larsen, Jack Lenor, and Weeks, Jeanne G. *Fabrics for Interiors*. New York: Van Nostrand Reinhold Co., 1975.

Lyle, Dorothy Siegert. *Performance of Textiles*. New York: John Wiley and Sons, Inc., 1977.

Moncrieff, R. W. *Man-Made Fibers*. New York: John Wiley and Sons, Inc., 1970.

Seiber, Roy. *African Textiles and Decorative Arts*. New York: Museum of Modern Art, 1972.

Seiler-Baldinger, Annemarie. *Systematik der Textilen Techniken*. Basler Beiträge zur Ethnologie Band 14, Pharos-Verlag Hansrudolf Schwabe A G. Basel, 1973.

Smith, Hervey Garrett. *The Arts of the Sailor*. New York: D. Van Nostrand Co., Inc., 1953.

Textile Fibers and Their Properties. Prepared by American Association for Textile Technology Council on Technology. Greensboro, NC: Burlington Industries, 1977.

Thorpe, Azalea Stuart, and Larsen, Jack Lenor. *Elements of Weaving*. rev. ed. Garden City, NY: Doubleday and Co., 1967.

West, Virginia M. *Finishing Touches for the Handweaver*. Newton Centre, MA: Charles T. Brandford Co., 1968.

Index

Page numbers in *italic* indicate photographs.

Abaca, 13
Alpaca, 18
Alternate crown sennit, 64
Alternate hitches, 64
Animal fibers, 8–9, 13, 16, 18–19
Apron, loom, 79, 82

Back beam
    defined, 79, 82
    working with, 92, 100
Balanced weave density
    art fabrics, *26–27, 40–41, 58–59, 70–71*
    discussed, 30, 38–39
    to figure warp length, 38, 124
Band forming edges, 68–69, 72
Bast fibers. *See* Hemp; Jute; Linen; Ramie
Beaming, 86, 91
    back to front, 91–95
    final stage, one person, 94–95
    final stage, two person, 95, 102
    front to back, 101–2
    sectional. *See* Sectional warping
Beater
    defined, 79, 81
    in use, 93, 95, 112, 118
    weighted, 83
Blanket stitching, 56, 57
Bouclé, 8
Bow knot, 97–98, 103
Braided edge
    forming a band, *54,* 68, 73
    with sennit fringe, 60–61
    simple sennit, *54,* 60, 64
Breast beam
    defined, 79, 82
    relationship to, 95, 111
Broken thread, to repair, 118–20
Brownlee-Ramsdale, Sandra, *Woodward Series #2, 80–81*

Camel's hair, 18
Cashmere, 18
Castle, 79, 92, 95, 98

Chained loops finish, 72, 73
Chenille, 8
Chokes, defined, 89
Cloth beam, defined, 79, 81, 82
Coir, 13
Continuous right crown sennit, 64
Cord-securing techniques, 65
Cotton, 9, 11
    burn test for, 123
    thread size, 23, 25
Creel, 105
Cross-stitching, 56, 57

Davis, Virginia, *Kasureru 8, 40–41*
Denier, 25
Dents, 81. *See also* Reed
Double knot finish, 72, 73
Double layer weaving, 35
    art fabrics, *66–67, 74–75, 80–81*
Double weaver's knot, 88, 108
Double wefting, 33
Dressing the loom
    defined, 85–86
    from back to front, 91–98
    from front to back, 91, 98–103, 117
    using sectional warp beam. *See* Sectional warping

Edge braiding, *54,* 72, 73
Eight-strand square sennit, 64

False knot, 94
Filament yarn, 8
Finishes, warp end, 55–56
    with fringes, 56–57, 60–61, 64–65
    without fringes, 68–69, 72–73
Fletcher, Mollie, *Apron, 74–75*
Four-strand sennit edge, 72, 73
Four-strand square sennit, 64
Forbes, Anne McCarthy, *Manta #4, 20–21*

Gimp, 8
Goat hair, 18
Guay, Nancy, *Sarahan I, 46–47*

Guide thread, 87, 105

Harnesses
    defined, 79, 81, 82
    position during beaming, 101
    position during tying up, 97
Heading, 112
Heddle hook
    defined, 83
    in use, 96, 97, 101
Heddles
    checking, 96, 100
    defined, 81, 82
    errors in threading, 112–14
    repair, metal or string, 112, 114
    threading, 96, 100, 101
Hemmed edge, *20, 36,* 55–56, *58–59*
Hemp, 12–13
Hemstitching, 57
Héon, Michelle, *Robe de Cérémonie 1, 70–71*
Horizontal clove hitches, 56
Horsehair, 18

Ikat (space dyeing), 33
    art fabrics, *36–37, 40–41, 62–63*

Jute, 13

Kente cloth, *28–29,* 35, 48
Kilim tabs, 60
Knauss, Lewis, *View from the Excelsior, 54–55*

Lamms, 79, 81
Lark's head, 60, 92, 107
Lary sticks
    defined, 91
    in use, 98, 99
Lease
    defined, 87, 91
    working with, 91, 92, 99–100
Lease sticks
    defined, 91
    in use, 91–92, 93, 98–99, 109

Lengthwise grain, 33
Linen, 9, 12
    burn test for, 123
    thread size, 23, 25
Llama, 18
Locked loop edge, 60, 61
Looms, 79–80
    considerations when using, 96, 97, 100, 101
    improvements to, 82–83
Looped edges, 60, 61

Manila hemp. *See* Abaca
Man-made fibers, 8–9, 19, 20–21
Maori edge, 72, 73
Marcoux, Alice, *Tyla's Blanket, 62–63*
Men's Weave: Kente Cloth (Ashanti), *28–29,* 35
Mercerization, 9
Metallic fibers, 22
    burn test for, 123
Metric conversions, 23
    reed size, 126
Mohair, 18

Narrow edge finishes, 72–73
Neolithic knot, 57
Novelty yarns, 8
Nylon, 9, 19, 22
    burn test for, 123
    thread size, 23, 25

Overcasting, 56, 57
Overhand knot, *26–27,* 57, 65, 107

Packing, 107
Painted warp, 33, *80–81*
Paper yarns, 13
Philippine edge, 60, 61
Plant fibers, 8–9, 12–13
Plied finish, *62,* 64
Ply, yarn, 8
Polypropylene, 22
    burn test for, 123
Posture, during weaving, 111–12

Pretzel tie, 93, 94

Raddle, 91
    in use, 92, 93, 97
Raffia, 13
Ramie, 12
Ratiné, 8
Rayon, 19
    burn test for, 123
    thread size, 23, 25
Reed, 79, 81, 82
    choice, 38, 125–26
    errors in threading, 112–16
    to sley, 96–97, 98–100
    in tension box, 105–9
    metric equivalents, 126
Reed hook, 83, 97
Reed marks, 38
Repeated half knots, 60
Rolf, Margot, *Starting from 4-Colors
    VII-13, 44–45*

Saran, 22
    burn test for, 123
Schira, Cynthia
    View to the East, 10–11
    warp experiment, *84–85*
Scholten, Herman
    Drie Bogen, 16–17
    Ruit, 58–59
Scholten van de Riviérè, Desirée
    Rode Stippen, 6–7
    Skyline, 24
Sectional warp beam
    defined, 104
    in use, 104–9
Sectional warping, 85, 103–9
Seelig, Warren
    Grosgrain Roll, 32
    Vertical Shield #2, 35, 66–67
Securing the warp (after winding),
    88–89
Selvedge treatments, 33, 42–43, *44–
    45*, 48
    to beam, 92, 98–99, 104, 106
Sennits, 60, 64
Shafts. *See* Harnesses
Shed, 79, 81

Shock absorbers, 79, 83
S-hook. *See* Reed hook
Shuttles, 83
Silk, 8, 18–19
    burn test for, 123
    thread size, 23, 25
Simple (fringeless) edge, 68, *70–71*
Sisal, 13
Skip plain weave, *52–53*
Sleying
    defined, 38
    to do, 96–97, 98–100
Slip knot, 96, 97, 99, 101
Slub yarn, 8
Soumak edge, 68, 69, 72
Spool rack, 105
Square knot, *26–27*, 60, 88, 101, 108
Staple fibers, 8
Stop knot, 97–98, 103
Stuffing, 118
Supplementary warp, 39, 41
    art fabrics with, *6–7, 20–21, 54,
    84–85*
Supplementary weft, 35, 42
    art fabrics with, *10–11, 14–15, 74–
    75, 84–85*
Swag (Wilson), *14–15,* 35

Taniko edge, 72
Tapestry, weft-face
    discussed, 49–53
    Peruvian, *50–51*
    Moroccan (rug), *52–53*
Tassels, 60
Tate, Blair
    Shadow Rows, 34
    Untitled, 26–27
Temple, 83, 121
Tex system, 25
Thomas, Jayn, *Wing Light, 36–37*
Tension box, 86, 104, 105–7
Threading draft, explained, 95, 100
Threading errors, 112–16
Threading pattern, defined, 81
Threading (process), 86
    heddles and reed, back to front,
    95–97
    heddles and reed, front to back,
    98–101

reed in tension box, 106–7
Treadles, 79
Treadling pattern, 81
Twined edge, 68, 69, 72
Twining, 56, 57
Tying up (process)
  back to front, 97–98
  front to back, 102–3
Tyla's Blanket (Marcoux), 33, *62–63*

Vertical clove hitches, 57
Vertical Shield #2 (Seelig), 35, *66–67*
Vicuna, 18

Warp
  adding a thread, 112, *114–15*
  chaining, 90–91
  density, 30–31. *See also* specific
    densities
  general discussion of, 3–4
  requirements for, 5, 7
Warp beam
  attaching warp to, 92, 101
  defined, 79, 82
  sectional. *See* Sectional warp beam
Warp brocade. *See* Supplementary
    warp
Warp-face balanced density, 30, 31,
    35–38
  art fabrics, *10–11, 28–29, 36–37,
    58–59*
  to figure warp length, 35, 124
Warp-face density, 30, 31, 33
  art fabrics, *14–15, 32, 34, 62–63*
  divided into layers, 35, *66–67, 74–
    75, 80–81*
  to figure warp length, 33, 124
  variations affecting, *14–15*, 33, *34*,
    35
  with weft-face weaving, *28–29*, 33,
    35, *62–63*
Warp guards, 107
Warping, 85, 86–91
Warping board, 86, 87
Warping paddles, 89–90, 93
Warping reel, 86, 87
Warp paper, 94, 102
Warp sticks, 91, 94–95, 102

Warp winding tricks, 89–90
Weaver's knot, 88, 108
Weaving
  defined, 3–4
  inserting the weft, 110–11, *119,
    120*, 121
  tension problems, 116–18
Weaving tools, 83
Weft
  general discussion of, 3–4
  to interweave. *See* Weaving
  relationship to warp. *See* specific
    densities
Weft brocade. *See* Supplementary
    weft
Weft-face balanced density, 30, 48–
    49
  art fabrics, *44–45, 46–47, 58–59*
  to figure warp length, 48, 124
Weft-face density, 30, 49–53
  art fabrics that include, *16–17, 24,
    28–29, 50–51, 52–53, 58–59,
    62–63, 70–71*
  to figure warp length, 49, 124
Whipping, 65
Wilson, Anne, *Swag, 14–15*, 35
Wire, 22–23
Wool, 13, 16, 18
  burn test for, 123
  thread size, 23
Woven edge finishes
  with fringe, 60, 61
  with cut ends, 68
  with sewn ends, 68–69, 72, *74*
Wrapping, *24*, 65

X, the, 87, 88–89

Yarn. *See also* Animal fibers; Man-
    made fibers; Plant fibers; specif-
    ic fibers
  general discussion of, 8–9
  requirements for warp, 5, 7
  size 23, 25

About the Author

Blair Tate is a textile artist and teacher. Her work has been exhibited widely, and has been included in shows at the Elements and Hadler/Rodriguez Gallery in New York, the La Jolla Museum of Contemporary Art in California, the Rose Art Museum and Thomas Segal Gallery in Boston, the American Academy in Rome, and the National Miniature Textile Exhibition at the Textile Museum in Washington, D.C. She was awarded Massachusetts Artists Foundation fellowships and a Bunting Fellowship from the Bunting Institute at Radcliffe College. She has created large-scale tapestries for site-specific architectural commissions, including One-Percent-for-Art public commissions in Connecticut and Massachusetts. She currently teaches in the textile department at the Rhode Island School of Design, of which she is a graduate.